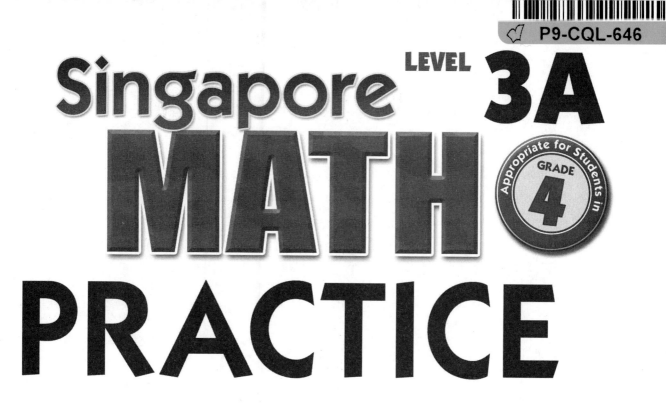

Singapore MATH PRACTICE

LEVEL 3A

Appropriate for Students in GRADE 4

Thinking Kids™
An imprint of Carson-Dellosa Publishing, LLC
Greensboro, North Carolina

P9-CQL-646

Visit carsondellosa.com for correlations to Common Core, state, national, and Canadian provincial standards.

Copyright © 2009 Singapore Asia Publishers PTE LTD.

Thinking Kids™
An imprint of Carson-Dellosa Publishing, LLC
PO Box 35665
Greensboro, NC 27425 USA

ISBN 978-0-7682-3993-5
03-214167784

INTRODUCTION TO SINGAPORE MATH

Welcome to Singapore Math! The math curriculum in Singapore has been recognized worldwide for its excellence in producing students highly skilled in mathematics. Students in Singapore have ranked at the top in the world in mathematics on the *Trends in International Mathematics and Science Study* (TIMSS) in 1993, 1995, 2003, and 2008. Because of this, Singapore Math has gained in interest and popularity in the United States.

Singapore Math curriculum aims to help students develop the necessary math concepts and process skills for everyday life and to provide students with the ability to formulate, apply, and solve problems. Mathematics in the Singapore Primary (Elementary) Curriculum cover fewer topics but in greater depth. Key math concepts are introduced and built-on to reinforce various mathematical ideas and thinking. Students in Singapore are typically one grade level ahead of students in the United States.

The following pages provide examples of the various math problem types and skill sets taught in Singapore.

At an elementary level, some simple mathematical skills can help students understand mathematical principles. These skills are the counting-on, counting-back, and crossing-out methods. Note that these methods are most useful when the numbers are small.

1. The Counting-On Method

Used for addition of two numbers. Count on in 1s with the help of a picture or number line.

$$7 + 4 = \mathbf{11}$$

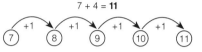

2. The Counting-Back Method

Used for subtraction of two numbers. Count back in 1s with the help of a picture or number line.

$$16 - 3 = \mathbf{13}$$

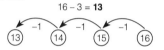

3. The Crossing-Out Method

Used for subtraction of two numbers. Cross out the number of items to be taken away. Count the remaining ones to find the answer.

$$20 - 12 = \mathbf{8}$$

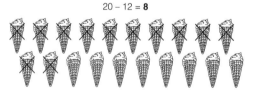

A **number bond** shows the relationship in a simple addition or subtraction problem. The number bond is based on the concept "part-part-whole." This concept is useful in teaching simple addition and subtraction to young children.

To find a whole, students must add the two parts.
To find a part, students must subtract the other part from the whole.

The different types of number bonds are illustrated below.

1. Number Bond (single digits)

3 (part) + 6 (part) = **9** (whole)

9 (whole) – 3 (part) = **6** (part)

9 (whole) – 6 (part) = **3** (part)

2. Addition Number Bond (single digits)

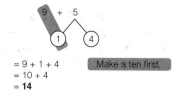

= 9 + 1 + 4 | Make a ten first. |
= 10 + 4
= **14**

3. Addition Number Bond (double and single digits)

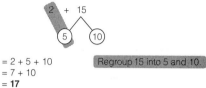

= 2 + 5 + 10 | Regroup 15 into 5 and 10. |
= 7 + 10
= **17**

4. Subtraction Number Bond (double and single digits)

10 – 7 = 3
3 + 2 = **5**

5. Subtraction Number Bond (double digits)

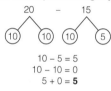

10 – 5 = 5
10 – 10 = 0
5 + 0 = **5**

Students should understand that multiplication is repeated addition and that division is the grouping of all items into equal sets.

1. Repeated Addition (Multiplication)

Mackenzie eats 2 rolls a day. How many rolls does she eat in 5 days?

$$2 + 2 + 2 + 2 + 2 = 10$$
$$5 \times 2 = 10$$

She eats **10** rolls in 5 days.

2. The Grouping Method (Division)

Mrs. Lee makes 14 sandwiches. She gives all the sandwiches equally to 7 friends. How many sandwiches does each friend receive?

$$14 \div 7 = 2$$

Each friend receives **2** sandwiches.

One of the basic but essential math skills students should acquire is to perform the 4 operations of whole numbers and fractions. Each of these methods is illustrated below.

1. The Adding-Without-Regrouping Method

```
H  T  O
3  2  1        O: Ones
+ 5  6  8      T: Tens
--------
8  8  9        H: Hundreds
```

Since no regrouping is required, add the digits in each place value accordingly.

2. The Adding-by-Regrouping Method

```
 H  T  O
 ¹4  9  2      O: Ones
+  1  5  3     T: Tens
--------
 6  4  5       H: Hundreds
```

In this example, regroup 14 tens into 1 hundred 4 tens.

Singapore Math Practice Level 3A

3. The Adding-by-Regrouping-Twice Method

$$\begin{array}{ccc} H & T & O \\ {}^{1}2 & {}^{1}8 & 6 \\ + 3 & 6 & 5 \\ \hline 6 & 5 & 1 \end{array}$$

O: Ones
T: Tens
H: Hundreds

Regroup twice in this example.
First, regroup 11 ones into 1 ten 1 one.
Second, regroup 15 tens into 1 hundred 5 tens.

4. The Subtracting-Without-Regrouping Method

$$\begin{array}{ccc} H & T & O \\ 7 & 3 & 9 \\ - 3 & 2 & 5 \\ \hline 4 & 1 & 4 \end{array}$$

O: Ones
T: Tens
H: Hundreds

Since no regrouping is required, subtract the digits in each place value accordingly.

5. The Subtracting-by-Regrouping Method

$$\begin{array}{ccc} H & T & O \\ 5 & {}^{7}8 & {}^{11}1 \\ - 2 & 4 & 7 \\ \hline 3 & 3 & 4 \end{array}$$

O: Ones
T: Tens
H: Hundreds

In this example, students cannot subtract 7 ones from 1 one. So, regroup the tens and ones. Regroup 8 tens 1 one into 7 tens 11 ones.

6. The Subtracting-by-Regrouping-Twice Method

$$\begin{array}{ccc} H & T & O \\ {}^{7}8 & {}^{9}0 & {}^{10}0 \\ - 5 & 9 & 3 \\ \hline 2 & 0 & 7 \end{array}$$

O: Ones
T: Tens
H: Hundreds

In this example, students cannot subtract 3 ones from 0 ones and 9 tens from 0 tens. So, regroup the hundreds, tens, and ones. Regroup 8 hundreds into 7 hundreds 9 tens 10 ones.

7. The Multiplying-Without-Regrouping Method

$$\begin{array}{cc} T & O \\ 2 & 4 \\ \times & 2 \\ \hline 4 & 8 \end{array}$$

O: Ones
T: Tens

Since no regrouping is required, multiply the digit in each place value by the multiplier accordingly.

8. The Multiplying-With-Regrouping Method

$$\begin{array}{ccc} H & T & O \\ {}^{1}3 & {}^{2}4 & 9 \\ \times & & 3 \\ \hline 1,0 & 4 & 7 \end{array}$$

O: Ones
T: Tens
H: Hundreds

In this example, regroup 27 ones into 2 tens 7 ones, and 14 tens into 1 hundred 4 tens.

9. The Dividing-Without-Regrouping Method

Since no regrouping is required, divide the digit in each place value by the divisor accordingly.

10. The Dividing-With-Regrouping Method

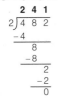

In this example, regroup 3 hundreds into 30 tens and add 3 tens to make 33 tens. Regroup 3 tens into 30 ones.

11. The Addition-of-Fractions Method

$$\frac{1 \times 2}{6 \times 2} + \frac{1 \times 3}{4 \times 3} = \frac{2}{12} + \frac{3}{12} = \frac{5}{12}$$

Always remember to make the denominators common before adding the fractions.

12. The Subtraction-of-Fractions Method

$$\frac{1 \times 5}{2 \times 5} - \frac{1 \times 2}{5 \times 2} = \frac{5}{10} - \frac{2}{10} = \frac{3}{10}$$

Always remembers to make the denominators common before subtracting the fractions.

13. The Multiplication-of-Fractions Method

$$\frac{{}^{1}\cancel{3}}{5} \times \frac{1}{{}_{3}\cancel{9}} = \frac{1}{15}$$

When the numerator and the denominator have a common multiple, reduce them to their lowest fractions.

14. The Division-of-Fractions Method

$$\frac{7}{9} \div \frac{1}{6} = \frac{7}{{}_{3}\cancel{9}} \times \frac{\cancel{6}^{2}}{1} = \frac{14}{3} = 4\frac{2}{3}$$

When dividing fractions, first change the division sign (÷) to the multiplication sign (×). Then, switch the numerator and denominator of the fraction on the right hand side. Multiply the fractions in the usual way.

Model drawing is an effective strategy used to solve math word problems. It is a visual representation of the information in word problems using bar units. By drawing the models, students will know of the variables given in the problem, the variables to find, and even the methods used to solve the problem.

Drawing models is also a versatile strategy. It can be applied to simple word problems involving addition, subtraction, multiplication, and division. It can also be applied to word problems related to fractions, decimals, percentage, and ratio.

The use of models also trains students to think in an algebraic manner, which uses symbols for representation.

The different types of bar models used to solve word problems are illustrated below.

1. The model that involves addition

Melissa has 50 blue beads and 20 red beads. How many beads does she have altogether?

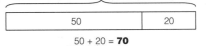

$50 + 20 = \mathbf{70}$

2. The model that involves subtraction

Ben and Andy have 90 toy cars. Andy has 60 toy cars. How many toy cars does Ben have?

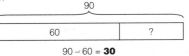

$90 - 60 = \mathbf{30}$

3. The model that involves comparison

Mr. Simons has 150 magazines and 110 books in his study. How many more magazines than books does he have?

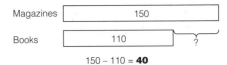

$150 - 110 = \mathbf{40}$

4. The model that involves two items with a difference

A pair of shoes costs $109. A leather bag costs $241 more than the pair of shoes. How much is the leather bag?

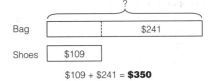

$109 + $241 = **$350**

5. The model that involves multiples

Singapore Math Practice Level 3A

Mrs. Drew buys 12 apples. She buys 3 times as many oranges as apples. She also buys 3 times as many cherries as oranges. How many pieces of fruit does she buy altogether?

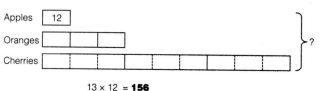

$$13 \times 12 = \mathbf{156}$$

6. The model that involves multiples and difference

There are 15 students in Class A. There are 5 more students in Class B than in Class A. There are 3 times as many students in Class C than in Class A. How many students are there altogether in the three classes?

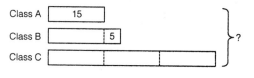

$$(5 \times 15) + 5 = \mathbf{80}$$

7. The model that involves creating a whole

Ellen, Giselle, and Brenda bake 111 muffins. Giselle bakes twice as many muffins as Brenda. Ellen bakes 9 fewer muffins than Giselle. How many muffins does Ellen bake?

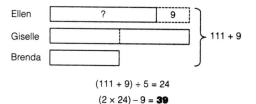

$$(111 + 9) \div 5 = 24$$
$$(2 \times 24) - 9 = \mathbf{39}$$

8. The model that involves sharing

There are 183 tennis balls in Basket A and 97 tennis balls in Basket B. How many tennis balls must be transferred from Basket A to Basket B so that both baskets contain the same number of tennis balls?

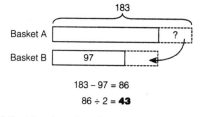

$$183 - 97 = 86$$
$$86 \div 2 = \mathbf{43}$$

9. The model that involves fractions

George had 355 marbles. He lost $\frac{1}{5}$ of the marbles and gave $\frac{1}{4}$ of the remaining marbles to his brother. How many marbles did he have left?

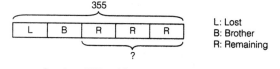

L: Lost
B: Brother
R: Remaining

5 parts → 355 marbles
1 part → 355 ÷ 5 = 71 marbles
3 parts → 3 × 71 = **213** marbles

10. The model that involves ratio

Aaron buys a tie and a belt. The prices of the tie and belt are in the ratio 2 : 5. If both items cost $539,

(a) what is the price of the tie?

(b) what is the price of the belt?

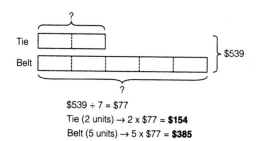

$$\$539 \div 7 = \$77$$
Tie (2 units) → 2 x $77 = **$154**
Belt (5 units) → 5 x $77 = **$385**

11. The model that involves comparison of fractions

Jack's height is $\frac{2}{3}$ of Leslie's height. Leslie's height is $\frac{3}{4}$ of Lindsay's height. If Lindsay is 160 cm tall, find Jack's height and Leslie's height.

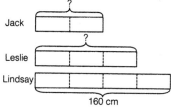

1 unit → 160 ÷ 4 = 40 cm

Leslie's height (3 units) → 3 × 40 = **120 cm**

Jack's height (2 units) → 2 × 40 = **80 cm**

Thinking skills and strategies are important in mathematical problem solving. These skills are applied when students think through the math problems to solve them. Below are some commonly used thinking skills and strategies applied in mathematical problem solving.

1. Comparing

Comparing is a form of thinking skill that students can apply to identify similarities and differences.

When comparing numbers, look carefully at each digit before deciding if a number is greater or less than the other. Students might also use a number line for comparison when there are more numbers.

Example:

3 is greater than 2 but smaller than 7.

2. Sequencing

A sequence shows the order of a series of numbers. *Sequencing* is a form of thinking skill that requires students to place numbers in a particular order. There are many terms in a sequence. The terms refer to the numbers in a sequence.

To place numbers in a correct order, students must first find a rule that generates the sequence. In a simple math sequence, students can either add or subtract to find the unknown terms in the sequence.

Example: Find the 7th term in the sequence below.

1,	4,	7,	10,	13,	16	?
1st term	2nd term	3rd term	4th term	5th term	6th term	7th term

Step 1: This sequence is in an increasing order.

Step 2: 4 − 1 = 3   7 − 4 = 3
The difference between two consecutive terms is 3.

Step 3: 16 + 3 = 19
The 7th term is **19**.

3. Visualization

Visualization is a problem solving strategy that can help students visualize a problem through the use of physical objects. Students will play a more active role in solving the problem by manipulating these objects.

The main advantage of using this strategy is the mobility of information in the process of solving the problem. When students make a wrong step in the process, they can retrace the step without erasing or canceling it.

The other advantage is that this strategy helps develop a better understanding of the problem or solution through visual objects or images. In this way, students will be better able to remember how to solve these types of problems.

Some of the commonly used objects for this strategy are toothpicks, straws, cards, strings, water, sand, pencils, paper, and dice.

4. Look for a Pattern

This strategy requires the use of observational and analytical skills. Students have to observe the given data to find a pattern in order to solve the problem. Math word problems that involve the use of this strategy usually have repeated numbers or patterns.

Example: Find the sum of all the numbers from 1 to 100.

Step 1: Simplify the problem.
Find the sum of 1, 2, 3, 4, 5, 6, 7, 8, 9, and 10.

Step 2: Look for a pattern.

1 + 10 = 11	2 + 9 = 11	3 + 8 = 11
4 + 7 = 11	5 + 6 = 11	

Step 3: Describe the pattern.
When finding the sum of 1 to 10, add the first and last numbers to get a result of 11. Then, add the second and second last numbers to get the same result. The pattern continues until all the numbers from 1 to 10 are added. There will be 5 pairs of such results. Since each addition equals 11, the answer is then 5 × 11 = 55.

Step 4: Use the pattern to find the answer.
Since there are 5 pairs in the sum of 1 to 10, there should be (10 × 5 = 50 pairs) in the sum of 1 to 100.
Note that the addition for each pair is not equal to 11 now. The addition for each pair is now (1 + 100 = 101).
50 × 101 = 5050
The sum of all the numbers from 1 to 100 is **5,050**.

5. Working Backward

The strategy of working backward applies only to a specific type of math word problem. These word problems state the end result, and students are required to find the total number. In order to solve these word problems, students have to work backward by thinking through the correct sequence of events. The strategy of working backward allows students to use their logical reasoning and sequencing to find the answers.

Example: Sarah has a piece of ribbon. She cuts the ribbon into 4 equal parts. Each part is then cut into 3 smaller equal parts. If the length of each small part is 35 cm, how long is the piece of ribbon?
3 × 35 = 105 cm
4 × 105 = 420 cm
The piece of ribbon is **420 cm**.

6. The Before-After Concept

The Before-After concept lists all the relevant data before and after an event. Students can then compare the differences and eventually solve the problems. Usually, the Before-After concept and the mathematical model go hand in hand to solve math word problems. Note that the Before-After concept can be applied only to a certain type of math word problem, which trains students to think sequentially.

Example: Kelly has 4 times as much money as Joey. After Kelly uses some money to buy a tennis racquet, and Joey uses $30 to buy a pair of pants, Kelly has twice as much money as Joey. If Joey has $98 in the beginning,
(a) how much money does Kelly have in the end?
(b) how much money does Kelly spend on the tennis racquet?

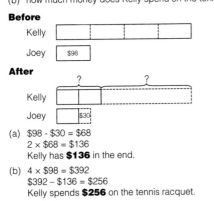

(a) $98 - $30 = $68
2 × $68 = $136
Kelly has **$136** in the end.

(b) 4 × $98 = $392
$392 - $136 = $256
Kelly spends **$256** on the tennis racquet.

7. Making Supposition

Making supposition is commonly known as "making an assumption." Students can use this strategy to solve certain types of math word problems. Making

assumptions will eliminate some possibilities and simplifies the word problems by providing a boundary of values to work within.

Example: Mrs. Jackson bought 100 pieces of candy for all the students in her class. How many pieces of candy would each student receive if there were 25 students in her class?

In the above word problem, assume that each student received the same number of pieces. This eliminates the possibilities that some students would receive more than others due to good behaviour, better results, or any other reason.

8. Representation of Problem

In problem solving, students often use representations in the solutions to show their understanding of the problems. Using representations also allow students to understand the mathematical concepts and relationships as well as to manipulate the information presented in the problems. Examples of representations are diagrams and lists or tables.

Diagrams allow students to consolidate or organize the information given in the problems. By drawing a diagram, students can see the problem clearly and solve it effectively.

A list or table can help students organize information that is useful for analysis. After analyzing, students can then see a pattern, which can be used to solve the problem.

9. Guess and Check

One of the most important and effective problem-solving techniques is *Guess and Check*. It is also known as *Trial and Error*. As the name suggests, students have to guess the answer to a problem and check if that guess is correct. If the guess is wrong, students will make another guess. This will continue until the guess is correct.

It is beneficial to keep a record of all the guesses and checks in a table. In addition, a *Comments* column can be included. This will enable students to analyze their guess (if it is too high or too low) and improve on the next guess. Be careful; this problem-solving technique can be tiresome without systematic or logical guesses.

Example: Jessica had 15 coins. Some of them were 10-cent coins and the rest were 5-cent coins. The total amount added up to $1.25. How many coins of each kind were there?

Use the guess-and-check method.

Number of 10¢ Coins	Value	Number of 5¢ Coins	Value	Total Number of Coins	Total Value
7	7 × 10¢ = 70¢	8	8 × 5¢ = 40¢	7 + 8 = 15	70¢ + 40¢ = 110¢ = $1.10
8	8 × 10¢ = 80¢	7	7 × 5¢ = 35¢	8 + 7 = 15	80¢ + 35¢ = 115¢ = $1.15
10	10 × 10¢ = 100¢	5	5 × 5¢ = 25¢	10 + 5 = 15	100¢ + 25¢ = 125¢ = $1.25

There were **ten** 10-cent coins and **five** 5-cent coins.

10. Restate the Problem

When solving challenging math problems, conventional methods may not be workable. Instead, restating the problem will enable students to see some challenging problems in a different light so that they can better understand them.

The strategy of restating the problem is to "say" the problem in a different and clearer way. However, students have to ensure that the main idea of the problem is not altered.

How do students restate a math problem?

First, read and understand the problem. Gather the given facts and unknowns. Note any condition(s) that have to be satisfied.

Next, restate the problem. Imagine narrating this problem to a friend. Present the given facts, unknown(s), and condition(s). Students may want to write the "revised" problem. Once the "revised" problem is analyzed, students should be able to think of an appropriate strategy to solve it.

11. Simplify the Problem

One of the commonly used strategies in mathematical problem solving is simplification of the problem. When a problem is simplified, it can be "broken down" into two or more smaller parts. Students can then solve the parts systematically to get to the final answer.

Singapore Math Practice Level 3A

Table of Contents

LEARNING OUTCOMES

Unit 1 Numbers 1–10,000

Students should be able to

- recognize and write numbers up to 10,000 in numerals and words.
- understand the place value of numbers up to 10,000.
- compare and arrange numbers up to 10,000.
- complete number patterns.

Unit 2 Adding Numbers up to 10,000

Students should be able to

- add numbers up to 10,000.
- perform addition by regrouping ones, tens, and hundreds.
- solve up to 2-step addition word problems.

Review 1

This review tests students' understanding of Units 1 & 2.

Unit 3 Subtracting Numbers up to 10,000

Students should be able to

- subtract numbers up to 10,000.
- perform subtraction by regrouping ones, tens, hundreds, and thousands.
- solve up to 2-step subtraction word problems.

Unit 4 Problem Solving (Adding and Subtracting)

Students should be able to

- solve up to 2-step word problems related to addition and subtraction.

Review 2

This review tests students' understanding of Units 3 & 4.

Unit 5 Multiplying Numbers by 6, 7, 8, and 9

Students should be able to

- multiply numbers by 6, 7, 8, and 9.
- divide numbers by 6, 7, 8, and 9.
- solve up to 2-step multiplication word problems.

Unit 6 Multiplying Numbers

Students should be able to

- multiply numbers without regrouping.
- multiply numbers by regrouping ones, tens, hundreds, and thousands.
- solve up to 2-step multiplication word problems.

Review 3

This review tests students' understanding of Units 5 & 6.

Unit 7 Dividing Numbers

Students should be able to

- divide numbers by regrouping hundreds, tens, and ones.
- find quotients and remainders by dividing.
- identify odd and even numbers.
- solve up to 2-step division word problems.

Unit 8 Problem Solving (Multiplying and Dividing)

Students should be able to

- solve up to 2-step word problems involving addition, subtraction, multiplication, and division.

Unit 9 Mental Calculations

Students should be able to

- mentally add and subtract two 2-digit numbers.
- mentally multiply and divide numbers within the multiplication table up to 10×10.

Review 4

This review tests students' understanding of Units 7, 8, & 9.

Final Review

This review is an excellent assessment of students' understanding of all the topics in this book.

Singapore Math Practice Level 3A

FORMULA SHEET

Unit 1 Numbers 1–10,000

4-digit numbers can be written in numerals or words.
Example: Write 8,945 in words.
eight thousand, nine hundred forty-five

<u>Place value</u>
In a 4-digit number, each digit has a different value. The place value is used to identify the particular place of a digit, such as thousands, hundreds, tens, or ones, and its value.

Example:
In 3,785,
the digit 3 is in the **thousands** place.
the digit 3 stands for **3,000**.
the value of the digit 3 is **3,000**.

<u>Comparing numbers</u>
Begin by comparing the 2 numbers from the thousands place.
- When one number is bigger than the other, use the words *greater than* to describe it.
- When one number is smaller than the other, use the words *smaller than* to describe it.

<u>Order and Pattern</u>
When arranging a set of numbers in order,
- determine if the series must begin with the largest or the smallest number,
- compare the place value of the numbers,
- arrange the numbers in the correct order.

For number pattern problems,
- determine if the number pattern is in an increasing or a decreasing order,
- find the difference between 2 consecutive numbers,
- apply the difference to find the unknown number.

More than and Less than
Replace the words *more than* with an addition sign (+).
Example: What is 1,000 more than 6,007?
1,000 + 6,007 = 7,007

Replace the words *less than* with a subtraction sign (–).
Example: What is 1,000 less than 6,007?
6,007 – 1,000 = 5,007

Unit 2 Adding Numbers up to 10,000

The word *sum* means addition.
<u>Adding without regrouping</u>
- Add the digits in the ones place first.
- Add the digits in the tens place.
- Add the digits in the hundreds place.
- Add the digits in the thousands place.

<u>Adding with regrouping</u>
- Add the digits in the ones place first. Regroup the ones if there are more than 10 ones.
- Add the digits in the tens place. Add another ten if there is a regrouping of ones. Regroup the tens if there are more than 10 tens.

- Add the digits in the hundreds place. Add another hundred if there is a regrouping of tens. Regroup the hundreds if there are more than 10 hundreds.
- Add the digits in the thousands place. Add another thousand if there is a regrouping of hundreds.

Unit 3 Subtracting Numbers up to 10,000

The word *difference* means subtraction.
<u>Subtracting without regrouping</u>
- Subtract the digits in the ones place first.
- Subtract the digits in the tens place.
- Subtract the digits in the hundreds place.
- Subtract the digits in the thousands place.

<u>Subtracting with regrouping</u>
- Subtract the digits in the ones place first. If this is not possible, regroup the tens and ones.
- Subtract the digits in the tens place. If this is not possible, regroup the hundreds and tens.
- Subtract the digits in the hundreds place. Regroup the thousands and hundreds if needed.
- Subtract the digits in the thousands place.

Unit 4 Problem Solving (Adding and Subtracting)

Below are suggested steps for solving addition and subtraction problems.

1. First, read and understand the problem.
2. Look for keywords to determine whether to add or subtract.
3. Draw models to help you understand the problem better.
4. Write the number sentences.
5. Remember to write your answers in the number sentences.
6. Write a statement to answer the word problem. You can underline the final answer in the statement.

Unit 5 Multiplying Numbers by 6, 7, 8, and 9

Below are the multiplication tables for 6, 7, 8, and 9.

×	6	7	8	9
1	6	7	8	9
2	12	14	16	18
3	18	21	24	27
4	24	28	32	36
5	30	35	40	45
6	36	42	48	54
7	42	49	56	63
8	48	56	64	72
9	54	63	72	81
10	60	70	80	90
11	66	77	88	99
12	72	84	96	108

Singapore Math Practice Level 3A

Unit 6 Multiplying Numbers

The terms in multiplication are:

multiplicand × multiplier = product

Multiplying without regrouping
- Multiply the digit in the ones place by the multiplier first.
- Multiply the digit in the tens place by the multiplier.
- Multiply the digit in the hundreds place by the multiplier.

Multiplying with regrouping
- Multiply the digit in the ones place by the multiplier first. Regroup the ones if there are more than 10 ones.
- Multiply the digit in the tens place by the multiplier. Remember to add the tens from the regrouping of ones if there are any. Regroup the tens if there are more than 10 tens.
- Multiply the digit in the hundreds place by the multiplier. Remember to add the hundreds from the regrouping of tens if there are any. Regroup the hundreds if there are more than 10 hundreds.

Unit 7 Dividing Numbers

The terms in division are:

dividend ÷ divisor = quotient and remainder

When the dividend can be divided equally by the divisor, there will be no remainder.

When the dividend cannot be divided equally by the divisor, there will be a remainder. The remainder will be less than the divisor.

Knowing the multiplication tables make division faster and easier.

Division without regrouping
- Divide the digit in the hundreds place by the divisor first.
- Divide the digit in the tens place by the divisor.
- Divide the digit in the ones place by the divisor.

Division with regrouping
- Divide the digit in the hundreds place by the divisor first. Find the remainder of hundreds if there is any.
- Regroup the remainder of hundreds to tens. Add up all tens. Divide the tens by the divisor. Find the remainder of tens if there is any.
- Regroup the remainder of tens to ones. Add up all ones. Divide the ones by the divisor. Find the remainder if there is any.

Odd numbers are numbers that will have a remainder of 1 when divided by 2.
Examples of odd numbers: 1, 3, 5, 7, 9, 11, ...

Even numbers are numbers that will have no remainder when divided by 2.
Examples of even numbers: 2, 4, 6, 8, 10, 12, ...

Unit 8 Problem Solving (Multiplying and Dividing)

Below are suggested steps for solving multiplication and division problems.

1. First, read and understand the problem.
2. Look for keywords to determine whether to multiply or divide.
3. Draw models to help you understand the problem better.
4. Write the number sentences.
5. Remember to write your answers in the number sentences.
6. Write a statement to answer the word problem. You can underline the final answer in the statement.

Unit 9 Mental Calculations

Adding mentally

Method 1
Step 1: Break up one of the addends into tens and ones.
Step 2: Add the other addend to the tens in Step 1.
Step 3: Add the remaining ones to the result in Step 2.

Method 2
Step 1: Round one of the addends to the nearest ten. Remember to find the difference between the addend and the rounded number.
Step 2: Add the rounded number to the other addend.
Step 3: Subtract the difference in Step 1 from the result obtained in Step 2.

Method 3
Step 1: Round one of the addends to 100. Remember to find the difference between the addend and 100.
Step 2: Add 100 to the other addend.
Step 3: Subtract the difference in Step 1 from the result obtained in Step 2.

Subtracting mentally

Method 1
Step 1: Break up one of the subtrahends into tens and ones.
Step 2: Subtract the tens in Step 1 from the other subtrahend.
Step 3: Subtract the remaining ones from the result obtained in Step 2.

Method 2
Step 1: Round one of the subtrahends to the nearest ten. Remember to find the difference between the subtrahend and the rounded number.
Step 2: Subtract the rounded number from the other subtrahend.
Step 3: Add the difference in Step 1 to the result obtained in Step 2.

Multiplying and Dividing mentally

In order to multiply and divide quickly and accurately, you must memorize the multiplication tables from 2 to 10.

When multiplying and dividing tens or hundreds by a number, substitute the zeros in the tens and hundreds the words *tens* or *hundreds*. This makes the numbers smaller and more manageable.

12

Unit 1: NUMBERS 1–10,000

Examples:

1. Write 3,208 in words. <u>three thousand, two hundred eight</u>

2. In 6,927,
   (a) the digit **2** is in the tens place.
   (b) the digit 9 is in the **hundreds** place.
   (c) the value of the digit **7** is 7.
   (d) the value of the digit 6 is **6,000**.
   (e) the digit 9 stands for **900**.

3. Arrange these numbers in order. Begin with the smallest.

   4,205, 3,761, 4,502, 6,389   <u>3,761, 4,205, 4,502, 6,389</u>

4. Complete the number pattern below.

   1,936, **2,036**, **2,136**, 2,236, 2,336, **2,436**

Write the numbers on the lines.

1. three thousand, six hundred twenty-five   _____

2. nine thousand, ninety-nine   _____

3. six thousand, two hundred eight   _____

4. five thousand, eight hundred seventeen   _____

5. eight thousand, thirty-five   _____

Singapore Math Practice Level 3A

Write the following numbers as words on the lines.

6. 9,693 _____

7. 4,313 _____

8. 8,440 _____

9. 7,015 _____

10. 6,505 _____

Count the numbers by tens, hundreds, or thousands. Write the correct answer in each blank.

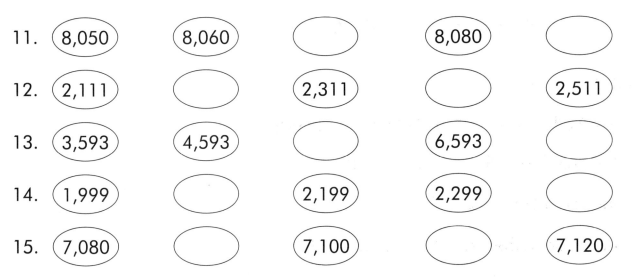

11. (8,050)   (8,060)   (   )   (8,080)   (   )

12. (2,111)   (   )   (2,311)   (   )   (2,511)

13. (3,593)   (4,593)   (   )   (6,593)   (   )

14. (1,999)   (   )   (2,199)   (2,299)   (   )

15. (7,080)   (   )   (7,100)   (   )   (7,120)

Fill in each blank with the correct answer.

16. 3,740 = _____ thousands _____ hundreds _____ tens _____ ones

17. 9,361 = _____ thousands _____ hundreds _____ tens _____ one

18. 7,001 = _____ thousands _____ hundreds _____ tens _____ one

19. 6,384 = _____ + _____ + _____ + _____

20. 1,072 = _____ + _____ + _____ + _____

Singapore Math Practice Level 3A

21. 4,951 = _____ + _____ + _____ + _____

22. 5,818 = 5,000 + _____ + 10 + 8

23. 2,756 = _____ + 700 + 50 + 6

24. 8,668 = 8,000 + _____ + 60 + 8

25. In 1,540,

    (a)   the digit _____ is in the ones place.

    (b)   the digit 1 is in the _____ place.

    (c)   the value of the digit 5 is _____.

    (d)   the value of the digit _____ is 40.

26. In 8,429,

    (a)   the digit _____ is in the hundreds place.

    (b)   the digit 9 is in the _____ place.

    (c)   the value of the digit 2 is _____.

    (d)   the value of the digit _____ is 8,000.

27. In 5,741,

    (a)   the digit _____ is in the thousands place.

    (b)   the digit 4 is in the _____ place.

    (c)   the value of the digit 7 is _____.

    (d)   the value of the digit _____ is 1.

Circle the smaller number in each pair.

28. 6,447   6,474

29. 1,704   1,047

30. 4,196   8,196

Circle the larger number in each pair.

31. 6,456   6,656

32. 8,294   8,942

33. 3,010   3,001

Circle the largest number in each set.

34. 4,614   4,216   4,461

35. 9,909   9,999   9,099

36. 5,115   5,515   5,551

Circle the smallest number in each set.

37. 8,624   2,468   2,648

38. 3,829   3,920   9,833

39. 5,625   6,250   2,056

Singapore Math Practice Level 3A

Fill in each blank with *greater* or *smaller*.

40. 1,068 is _____ than 1,168.

41. 8,843 is _____ than 8,803.

42. 7,452 is _____ than 5,252.

43. 3,090 is _____ than 309.

44. 4,234 is _____ than 4,324.

Complete the number patterns.

45. 1,540, 1,545, _____, _____, 1,560

46. 4,869, _____, 4,669, 4,569, _____

47. 2,330, 2,340, _____, 2,360, _____

48. 8,719, _____, _____, 5,719, 4,719

49. 5,876, 5,886, _____, _____, 5,916

Arrange the following numbers in order. Begin with the largest.

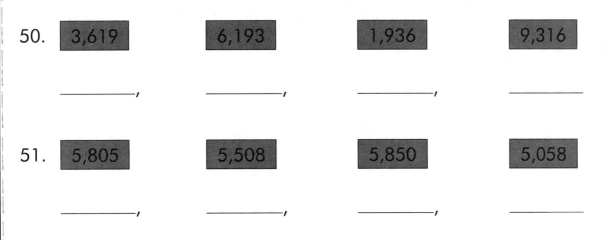

50. 3,619   6,193   1,936   9,316

_____, _____, _____, _____

51. 5,805   5,508   5,850   5,058

_____, _____, _____, _____

Singapore Math Practice Level 3A

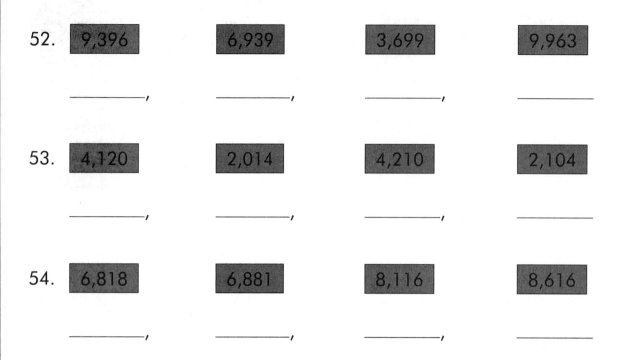

52. 9,396   6,939   3,699   9,963

_____,   _____,   _____,   _____

53. 4,120   2,014   4,210   2,104

_____,   _____,   _____,   _____

54. 6,818   6,881   8,116   8,616

_____,   _____,   _____,   _____

Arrange the following numbers in order. Begin with the smallest.

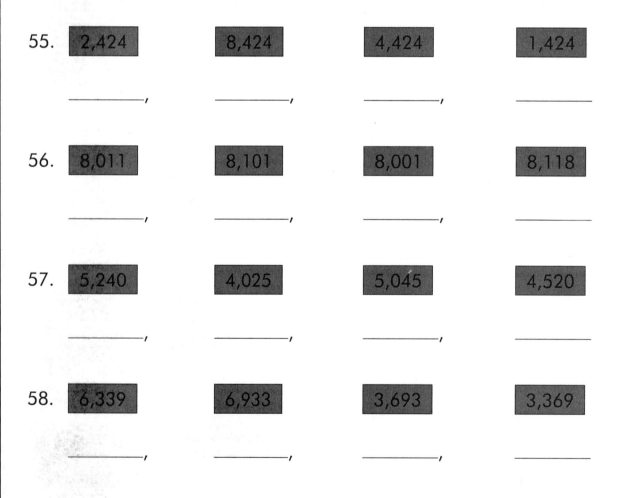

55. 2,424   8,424   4,424   1,424

_____,   _____,   _____,   _____

56. 8,011   8,101   8,001   8,118

_____,   _____,   _____,   _____

57. 5,240   4,025   5,045   4,520

_____,   _____,   _____,   _____

58. 6,339   6,933   3,693   3,369

_____,   _____,   _____,   _____

Singapore Math Practice Level 3A

59.

_____, _____, _____, _____

60. What is the largest 4-digit number you can make using the digits 6, 2, 8, and 1?

_____

61. What is the smallest 4-digit number you can make using the digits 9, 3, 5, and 7?

_____

Singapore Math Practice Level 3A

Unit 2: ADDING NUMBERS UP TO 10,000

Examples:

1. Find the sum of 5,420 and 3,519.

$$\begin{array}{r} 5{,}4\,2\,0 \\ +\ 3{,}5\,1\,9 \\ \hline 8{,}9\,3\,9 \end{array}$$

2. Find the sum of 2,847 and 4,753.

$$\begin{array}{r} \overset{1\ \ 1\ \ 1}{2{,}8\,4\,7} \\ +\ 4{,}7\,5\,3 \\ \hline 7{,}6\,0\,0 \end{array}$$

Find the sum of the following numbers.

1. 1,386 and 2,001 = _____

2. 5,210 and 4,689 = _____

3. 4,037 and 2,232 = _____

4. 6,512 and 3,076 = _____

5. 4,378 and 1,521 = _____

Fill in each blank with the correct answer.

6. 3 hundreds 6 tens + 8 hundreds 3 tens

    = ____ hundreds ____ tens

    = ____ thousand ____ hundred ____ tens

Singapore Math Practice Level 3A

7. 5 hundreds 9 tens 3 ones + 6 hundreds 4 tens 2 ones

= ____ hundreds ____ tens ____ ones

= ____ thousand ____ hundreds ____ tens ____ ones

8. 7 hundreds 6 tens 9 ones + 5 hundreds 2 tens 4 ones

= ____ hundreds ____ tens ____ ones

= ____ thousand ____ hundreds ____ tens ____ ones

9. 4 hundreds 2 tens 5 ones + 8 hundreds 8 tens 9 ones

= ____ hundreds ____ tens ____ ones

= ____ thousand ____ hundreds ____ ten ____ ones

10. 9 hundreds 1 ten 5 ones + 8 hundreds 5 tens

= ____ hundreds ____ tens ____ ones

= ____ thousand ____ hundreds ____ tens ____ ones

Fill in each blank with the correct answer.

11. The sum of 2,790 and 5,637 is _____.

12. The sum of 4,078 and 3,659 is _____.

13. The sum of 8,316 and 1,473 is _____.

Singapore Math Practice Level 3A

Add the following numbers. Show your work.

14.   1,7 4 5
      + 6,4 8 7
      _____

19.   2,2 8 2
      + 5,4 1 3
      _____

15.   8,4 0 0
      + 1,3 2 4
      _____

20.   4,9 0 8
      + 1,7 6 7
      _____

16.   3,3 5 6
      + 4,1 3 4
      _____

21.   6,2 1 0
      + 1,5 3 8
      _____

17.   4,3 4 8
      + 1,6 2 5
      _____

22.   9,1 2 6
      +   1 4 2
      _____

18.   7,4 3 0
      + 1,9 3 2
      _____

23.   4,8 1 3
      + 4,1 3 5
      _____

Singapore Math Practice Level 3A

24.
$$5,410$$
$$+\ 2,385$$

29.
$$6,281$$
$$+\ 1,198$$

25.
$$3,869$$
$$+\ 2,435$$

30.
$$4,633$$
$$+\ 3,047$$

26.
$$3,863$$
$$+\ 5,576$$

31.
$$2,282$$
$$+\ 4,060$$

27.
$$5,657$$
$$+\ 3,638$$

32.
$$3,632$$
$$+\ 6,261$$

28.
$$5,375$$
$$+\ 2,917$$

Match each butterfly to the correct flower.

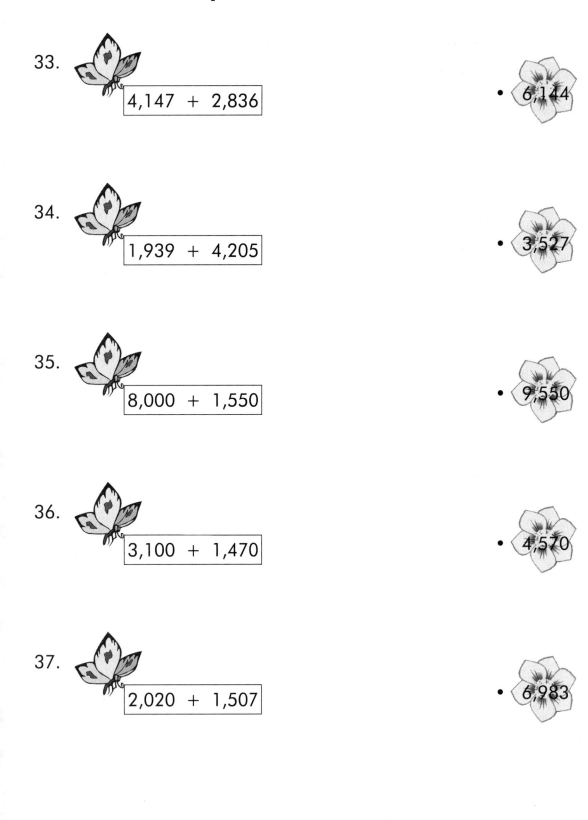

33. 4,147 + 2,836

34. 1,939 + 4,205

35. 8,000 + 1,550

36. 3,100 + 1,470

37. 2,020 + 1,507

• 6,144

• 3,527

• 9,550

• 4,570

• 6,983

Singapore Math Practice Level 3A

Solve the following word problems. Show your work in the space below.

38. Shop A sells 3,279 cans of drinks. Shop B sells 2,580 cans of drinks. How many cans of drinks do both shops sell altogether?

39. Sam spent $1,574 in January. He spent $3,100 in February. How much did he spend altogether?

40. Jerry, a truck driver, traveled 4,200 km in June. He travelled 1,935 km more in July. How far did he travel in July?

41. Ben collects 4,164 bottle caps. William collects 2,659 bottle caps more than Ben. How many bottle caps does William collect?

42. Tomás sold 2,347 pens in February. He sold 3,169 pens in March. How many pens did he sell in the 2 months?

Singapore Math Practice Level 3A

REVIEW 1

Write the following numbers as words on the lines.

1. 1,915 _____

2. 6,306 _____

Write the numbers on the lines.

3. three thousand, twelve   _____

4. eight thousand, two hundred twenty-eight   _____

Add the following numbers. Show your work.

5.   4,3 7 9
     + 2,4 6 8
     _____

7.   5,3 8 5
     + 2,4 1 8
     _____

6.   1,0 0 2
     + 2,8 9 9
     _____

8.   4,0 1 6
     + 3,8 4 9
     _____

Circle the smaller number in each pair.

9. 4,879   4,798

10. 1,050   1,500

Circle the largest number in each set.

11. 3,711   3,177   3,717

12. 6,023   6,203   6,032

Complete the number patterns.

13. 4,614, 4,624, _____, _____, 4,654

14. 7,899, _____, 7,937, 7,956, _____

Arrange the following numbers in order. Begin with the smallest.

15.

_____,   _____,   _____,   _____

Fill in each blank with the correct answer.

16. In 2,036,

   (a) the digit _____ is in the thousands place.

   (b) the value of the digit 6 is _____.

   (c) the digit 0 is in the _____ place.

   (d) the value of the digit _____ is 30.

17. The sum of 7,096 and 1,845 is _____.

18. 4 hundreds 3 tens 4 ones + 9 hundreds 1 ten 5 ones

    = _____ hundreds _____ tens _____ ones

    = _____ thousand _____ hundreds _____ tens _____ ones

Solve the following word problems. Show your work in the space below.

19. Kwame saved $4,312 in March. He saved $688 more in April than in March. How much did he save in April?

20. Mandy pays $1,375 for a diamond bracelet. She pays $1,999 more for a diamond necklace. How much does Mandy pay for the diamond necklace?

Unit 3: SUBTRACTING NUMBERS UP TO 10,000

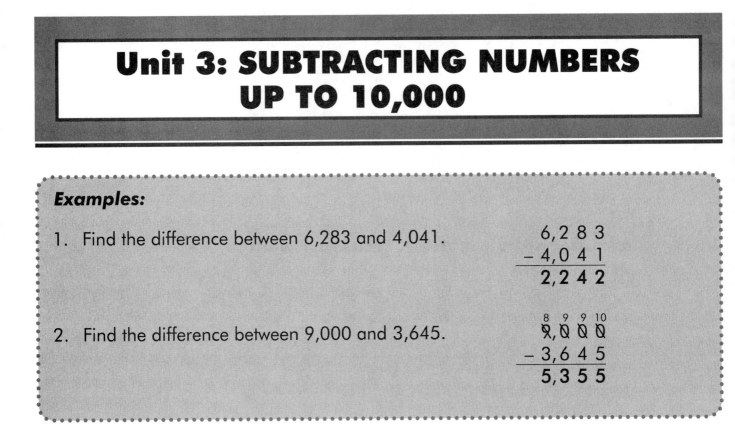

Examples:

1. Find the difference between 6,283 and 4,041.

$$\begin{array}{r} 6,283 \\ -\ 4,041 \\ \hline 2,242 \end{array}$$

2. Find the difference between 9,000 and 3,645.

$$\begin{array}{r} {}^{8}\ {}^{9}\ {}^{9}\ {}^{10} \\ \cancel{9},\cancel{0}\cancel{0}\cancel{0} \\ -\ 3,645 \\ \hline 5,355 \end{array}$$

Find the difference between the following numbers.

1. 67 and 17 = _____

2. 53 and 12 = _____

3. 548 and 320 = _____

4. 486 and 35 = _____

5. 979 and 546 = _____

Singapore Math Practice Level 3A

Solve the following subtraction problems. Show your work.

6.   3,8 6 9
    −   2 3 5
    _____

7.   7,7 8 7
    − 4,3 2 5
    _____

8.   9,7 7 6
    − 1,0 8 5
    _____

9.   5,8 8 1
    − 4,0 5 8
    _____

10.   2,9 0 0
     −   8 9 0
     _____

11.   4,1 3 6
     − 2,1 2 8
     _____

12.   6,8 4 8
     − 2,0 0 5
     _____

13.   2,4 2 6
     − 1,3 1 0
     _____

14.   7,4 3 1
     − 5,6 1 1
     _____

15.   8,8 1 8
     − 7,1 0 7
     _____

16.   9,1 3 0
     − 3,6 8 4
     _____

17.   8,2 9 2
     − 2,5 0 5
     _____

Singapore Math Practice Level 3A

18.　5,3 9 2
　　 − 2,8 8 6

22.　8,0 0 0
　　 − 4,6 5 9

19.　4,9 8 8
　　 − 3,9 6 9

23.　3,5 7 6
　　 − 1,8 9 9

20.　9,3 6 8
　　 − 1,4 8 7

24.　6,0 0 5
　　 − 4,7 6 9

21.　2,3 7 6
　　 − 1,4 8 7

25.　8,0 1 0
　　 − 3,8 6 5

Fill in each blank with the correct answer.

26.　4,369 − 3,124 = _____

27.　5,139 − 2,000 = _____

28.　5,353 − 1,526 = _____

29.　3,350 − 1,598 = _____

30.　6,206 − 2,062 = _____

Singapore Math Practice Level 3A

31. Cameron is expecting a gift from his father. Solve the subtraction problems, and write the correct letter in each box to reveal the gift Cameron gets from his father.

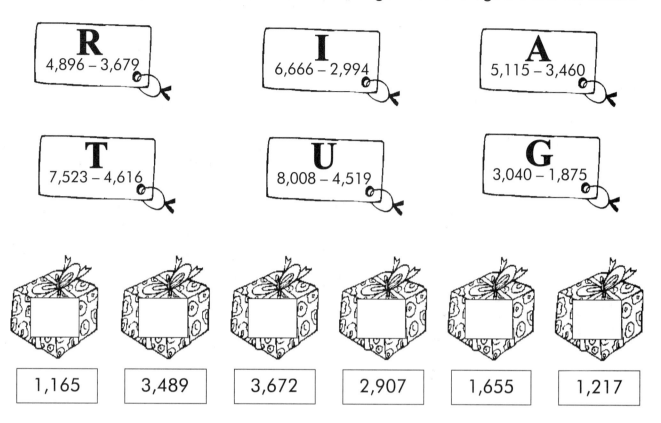

R	I	A
4,896 – 3,679	6,666 – 2,994	5,115 – 3,460

T	U	G
7,523 – 4,616	8,008 – 4,519	3,040 – 1,875

| 1,165 | 3,489 | 3,672 | 2,907 | 1,655 | 1,217 |

Solve the following word problems. Show your work in the space below.

32. Hafiz has 4,376 stickers in his collection. Alex has 2,950 fewer stickers. How many stickers does Alex have?

$$
\begin{array}{r}
{\scriptstyle 3\ 13} \\
4\,\cancel{3}\cancel{7}6 \\
-\ 2\,950 \\
\hline
1\,426
\end{array}
$$

Alex has 1426 stickers.

Singapore Math Practice Level 3A

33. Amelia uses 2,315 beads to make a necklace. She uses 1,670 beads to make a bracelet. How many fewer beads does she use for the bracelet?

34. Alicia baked 5,300 muffins in June. She baked 565 fewer muffins in July. How many muffins did Alicia bake in July?

35. LaTonya pays $6,478 for a television set. She pays $2,590 less for a laptop. How much does the laptop cost?

36. Rosa sold some stamps on Monday. She sold 4,825 stamps on Tuesday. The total number of stamps she sold on these 2 days was 9,000. How many stamps did she sell on Monday?

Unit 4: PROBLEM SOLVING (ADDING AND SUBTRACTING)

Examples:

1. Jessie bought a purse for $999. She bought a dress for $199. How much did she spend altogether?

    Solution:

    The keyword *altogether* suggests that we should add the 2 numbers.

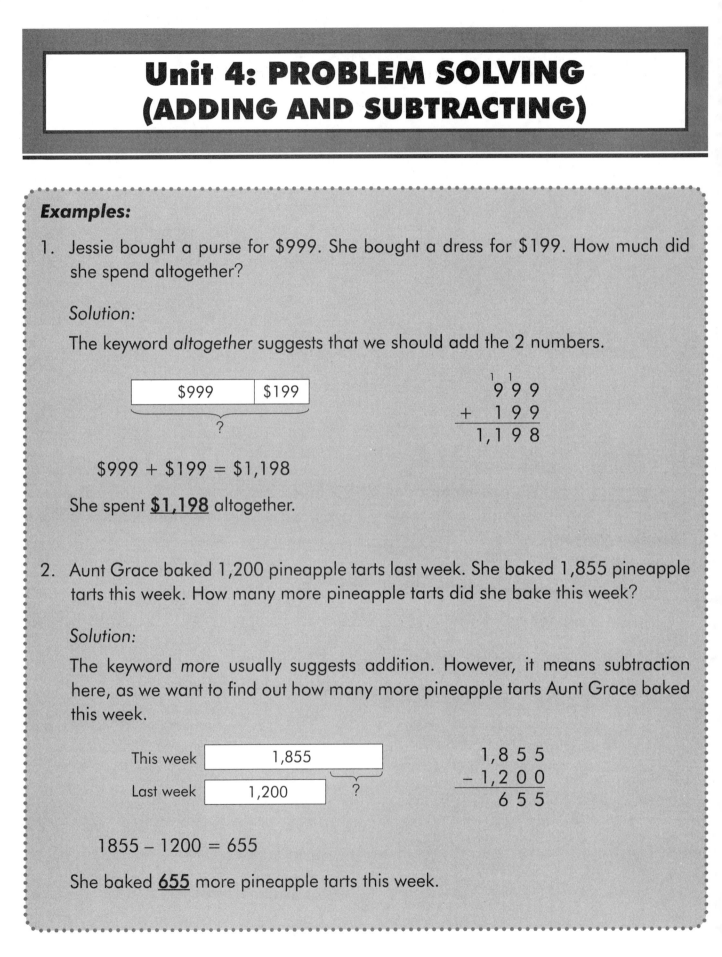

    $999 + $199 = $1,198

    She spent **$1,198** altogether.

2. Aunt Grace baked 1,200 pineapple tarts last week. She baked 1,855 pineapple tarts this week. How many more pineapple tarts did she bake this week?

    Solution:

    The keyword *more* usually suggests addition. However, it means subtraction here, as we want to find out how many more pineapple tarts Aunt Grace baked this week.

    1855 − 1200 = 655

    She baked **655** more pineapple tarts this week.

Solve the following word problems. Show your work in the space below.

1. Mia has 236 stickers. Abby has 127 fewer stickers than Mia.

   (a) How many stickers does Abby have?

   (b) How many stickers do they have altogether?

2. Roberto travels 3,280 mi. on his motorcycle. Steve travels 568 mi. farther than Roberto. How far do they travel altogether?

3. Hailey has 2,345 stamps in her collection. Asia has 3,542 stamps in her collection.

(a) How many more stamps does Asia have than Hailey?

(b) How many stamps do they have altogether?

4. Sarah earns $2,140 a month. Carmen earns $150 more than Sarah. Sonya earns $270 less than Carmen. How much does Sonya earn?

5. Rebecca pays $2,080 for her television set. Kimiko pays $275 less for her television

set.

(a) How much does Kimiko pay for her television set?

(b) How much do both television sets cost?

6. 3,865 girls went to a concert. 1,459 more boys went to the same concert. How many children went to the concert altogether?

7. 2,015 people attended a carnival on Saturday. 3,585 more people attended the carnival on Sunday. How many people attended the carnival on both days?

8. Jason used 1,075 kg of cement to build a house on Monday. He used 360 kg less cement on Tuesday. How much cement did he use on both days?

9. A used van costs $5,180. It costs $3,960 to buy a used motorcycle.

    (a) How much less is the used motorcycle than the used van?

    (b) How much will it cost to buy the used van and the used motorcycle?

10. Alexandra spent $2,387 on books and school supplies last year. Her parents asked her to spend $500 less this year.

(a) How much could Alexandra spend on books and school supplies this year?

(b) If Alexandra were to spend $4,000 on books and school supplies this year, how much would she have overspent?

REVIEW 2

Solve the following subtraction problems. Show your work.

1.   9,3 6 8
    − 1,4 0 9

3.   8,1 1 1
    − 2,4 0 1

2.   4,7 5 5
    − 1,8 9 0

4.   6,0 0 0
    − 2,8 1 9

Write the missing number in each box.

5.   9,5 ☐ 6
    − 3,7 8 9
       5,7 4 7

6.   ☐,5 4 4
    − 1,1 7 3
       4,3 7 1

Fill in each blank with the correct answer.

7. Find the difference between 6,865 and 2,648.   _____

8. 2,865 − 1,750 = ☐   _____

9. Subtract 1,011 from 5,900.   _____

10. 4,000 − 100 = ☐   _____

Singapore Math Practice Level 3A

11. Subtract 10 from 6,940.   _____

12. Find the difference between 8,000 and 450.   _____

13. 5,050 is 500 less than [   ].   _____

14. Solve the following problems to find Timothy's favorite sandwich.

R	6,3 8 9 − 4,6 9 3	T	2,4 1 5 + 1,5 9 6
E	8,2 0 0 − 3,8 6 5	A	5,1 8 9 + 2,6 9 0
U	3,4 8 7 − 1,5 0 9	B	4,4 4 4 + 2,0 5 5
N	7,7 7 7 − 5,9 9 8	P	1,0 9 0 + 2,8 9 5

[ ]	[ ]	[ ]	[ ]	[ ]	[ ]
3,985	4,335	7,879	1,779	1,978	4,011

[ ]	[ ]	[ ]	[ ]	[ ]	[ ]
6,499	1,978	4,011	4,011	4,335	1,696

Singapore Math Practice Level 3A

Solve the following word problems. Show your work in the space below.

15. Sophia earns $2,470 a month. June earns $2,745 a month.

    (a) How much more money does June earn than Sophia?

    (b) How much do they earn altogether?

16. Yoko has 2,100 stamps in her collection. Andrew has 1,900 more stamps than Yoko. How many stamps do they have altogether?

17. Shop A sells 4,985 T-shirts in a month. Shop B sells 1,200 T-shirts more than Shop A. Shop C sells 2,350 fewer T-shirts than Shop B. How many T-shirts does Shop C sell?

18. Jake has 3,967 stickers. His brother gives him another 450 stickers. Jake then gives 1,050 stickers to his friends. How many stickers does Jake have left?

19. Raj drove 4,745 mi. in August. He drove 2,080 mi. less in September than in August. Find Raj's total driving distance in these 2 months.

20. Isaiah used 5,000 wooden blocks to build a castle. He used 4,360 fewer wooden blocks to build a house.

(a) How many wooden blocks did he use to build the house?

(b) How many wooden blocks did he use altogether?

Unit 5: MULTIPLYING NUMBERS BY 6, 7, 8, AND 9

Examples:

1. $8 \times 6 = \underline{48}$

2. $5 \times 7 = \underline{35}$

3. $8 \times 8 = \underline{64}$

4. $9 \times 3 = \underline{27}$

Fill in each blank with the correct answer.

1. $2 \times 6 = $ _____

2. 5 sixes $= $ _____

3. _____ $\times 8 = 80$

4. _____ $\times 7 = 56$

5. $9 \times 9 = $ _____

6. _____ $\times 8 = 40$

7. 4 eights $= $ _____

8. _____ $\times 6 = 24$

9. 3 sevens $= $ _____

10. $7 \times 7 = $ _____

11. $5 \times 9 = $ _____

12. _____ $\times 9 = 72$

Singapore Math Practice Level 3A

13. _____ × 8 = 64

14. _____ × 8 = 48

15. 9 × 0 = _____

Match each steering wheel to the correct car.

16. 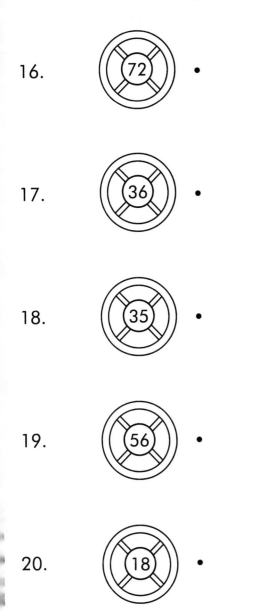 •

•

17. •

•

18. •

•

19. •

•

20. •

•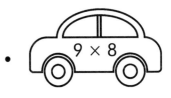

Solve the following multiplication problems using the short-cut method.

21. (a) 7 × 7 = 35 + ___ + ___

                    = 35 + ___

                    = ___

  (b) 8 × 6 = 30 + ___ + ___ + ___

                    = 30 + ___

                    = ___

  (c) 8 × 8 = 40 + ___ + ___ + ___

                    = 40 + ___

                    = ___

22. (a) 9 × 8 = ___ – ___

                    = ___

  (b) 9 × 6 = ___ – ___

                    = ___

Singapore Math Practice Level 3A

Study the pictures carefully. Fill in each blank with the correct answer.

23.

There are _____ groups of helmets.

There are _____ helmets in each group.

There are _____ helmets altogether.

24.

There are _____ groups of T-shirts.

There are _____ T-shirts in each group.

There are _____ T-shirts altogether.

Singapore Math Practice Level 3A

25.

There are _____ groups of socks.

There are _____ socks in each group.

There are _____ socks altogether.

26.

There are _____ groups of spoons.

There are _____ spoons in each group.

There are _____ spoons altogether.

Singapore Math Practice Level 3A

27.

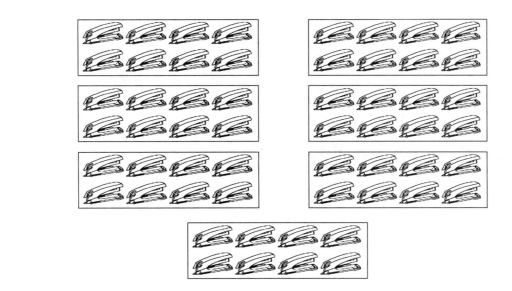

There are _____ groups of staplers.

There are _____ staplers in each group.

There are _____ staplers altogether.

Look at the pictures carefully. Write 2 multiplication and division sentences for each set of pictures.

28.

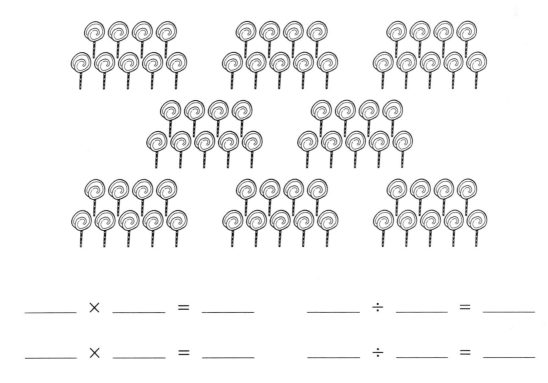

_____ × _____ = _____   _____ ÷ _____ = _____

_____ × _____ = _____   _____ ÷ _____ = _____

Singapore Math Practice Level 3A

29.

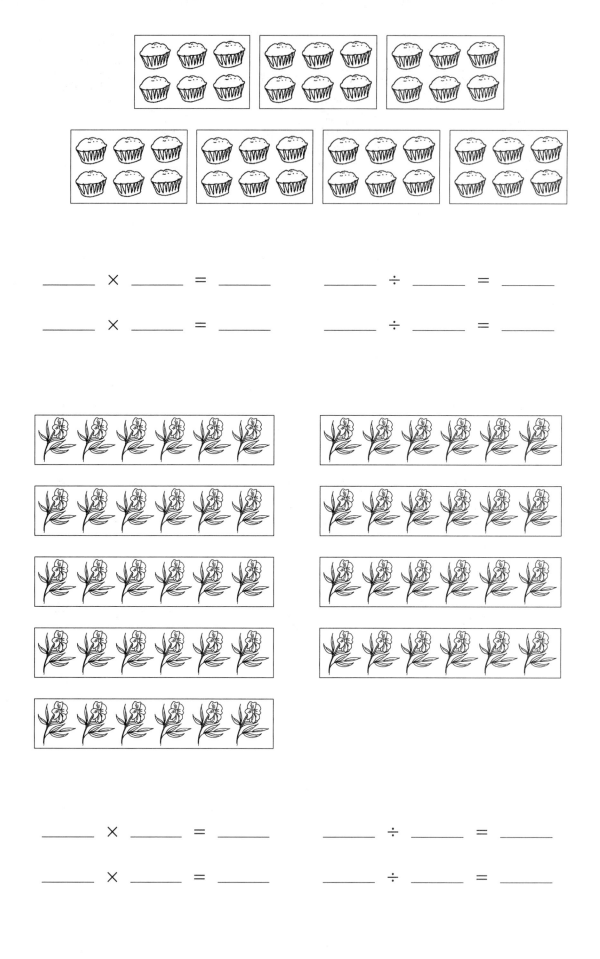

_____ × _____ = _____   _____ ÷ _____ = _____

_____ × _____ = _____   _____ ÷ _____ = _____

30.

_____ × _____ = _____   _____ ÷ _____ = _____

_____ × _____ = _____   _____ ÷ _____ = _____

Singapore Math Practice Level 3A

31.

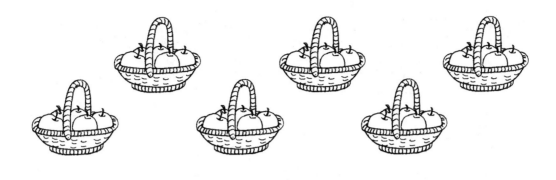

_____ × _____ = _____   _____ ÷ _____ = _____

_____ × _____ = _____   _____ ÷ _____ = _____

32.

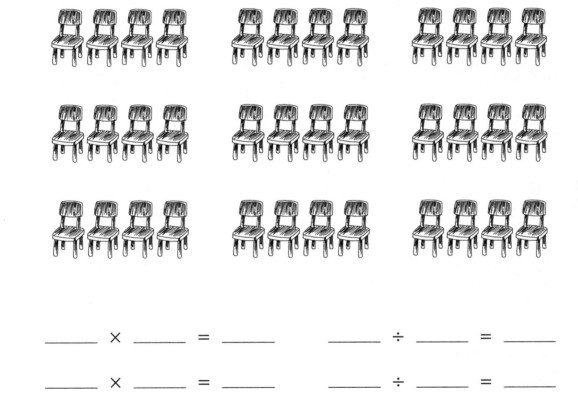

_____ × _____ = _____   _____ ÷ _____ = _____

_____ × _____ = _____   _____ ÷ _____ = _____

Singapore Math Practice Level 3A

Solve the following word problems. Show your work in the space below.

33. Samantha bought 6 bags of oranges. There were 8 oranges in each bag. How many oranges did she buy altogether?

34. Andy buys 5 books at a bookshop. If each book costs $6, how much does Andy pay for all the books?

Singapore Math Practice Level 3A

35. A group of people are going to the zoo by car. They need 7 cars altogether. If 5 people sit in each car, how many people are there in the group?

36. Elizabeth bakes 9 trays of muffins. There are 8 muffins on each tray. How many muffins does Elizabeth bake altogether?

37. Enzo has 42 stickers. He shares these stickers with 6 friends. How many stickers does each of them have?

38. Mrs. Arnold bought 64 apples. She put them equally into 8 bags. How many apples were there in each bag?

Unit 6: MULTIPLYING NUMBERS

Examples:

1.
```
     1 1
   ×   7
   ─────
     7 7
```

2.
```
    ⁴3 5
   ×   8
   ─────
   2 8 0
```

3.
```
     2 1 0
   ×     3
   ───────
     6 3 0
```

4.
```
   ¹ ³4 2 5
   ×       6
   ─────────
   2,5 5 0
```

Solve the following multiplication problems. Show your work.

1.
```
     1 2
   ×   3
   ─────
```

2.
```
     1 1 2
   ×     4
   ───────
```

3.
```
     3 3
   ×   2
   ─────
```

4.
```
     2 1 0
   ×     2
   ───────
```

5.
```
     3 0 2
   ×     3
   ───────
```

6.
```
     4 4 2
   ×     2
   ───────
```

7.
```
     2 1 2
   ×     4
   ───────
```

8.
```
     3 1
   ×   3
   ─────
```

9.
```
     1 0 0
   ×     3
   ───────
```

10.
```
     1 2 1
   ×     4
   ───────
```

59

Match each door to the correct house.

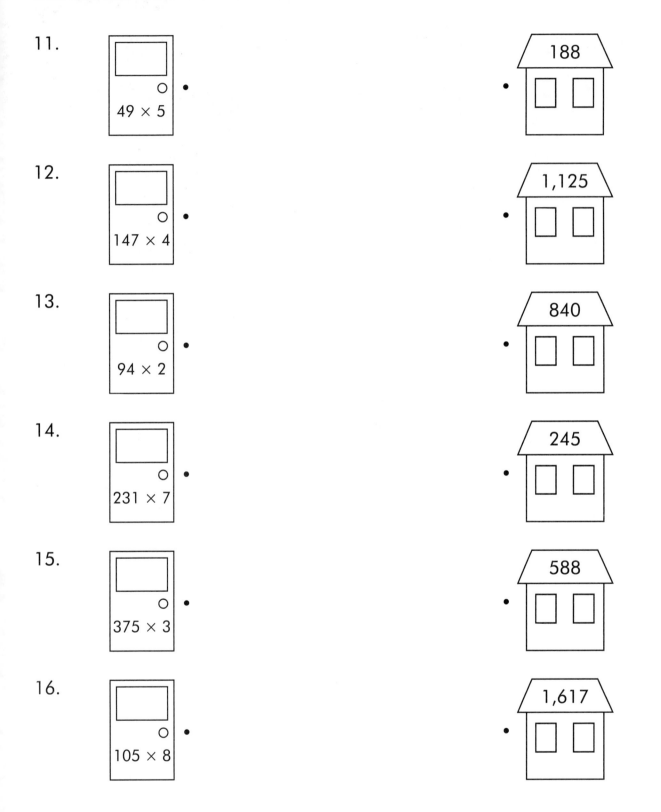

11. 49×5

12. 147×4

13. 94×2

14. 231×7

15. 375×3

16. 105×8

188

1,125

840

245

588

1,617

Fill in each box with the correct answer.

17.

	Across		**Down**
(a)	112 × 8	(f)	91 × 7
(b)	79 × 9	(g)	102 × 6
(c)	62 × 5	(h)	46 × 8
(d)	214 × 4	(i)	98 × 9
(e)	118 × 7	(j)	80 × 8

Singapore Math Practice Level 3A

Sandra is at the circus with her family. Find out who her favorite performer is.

18.

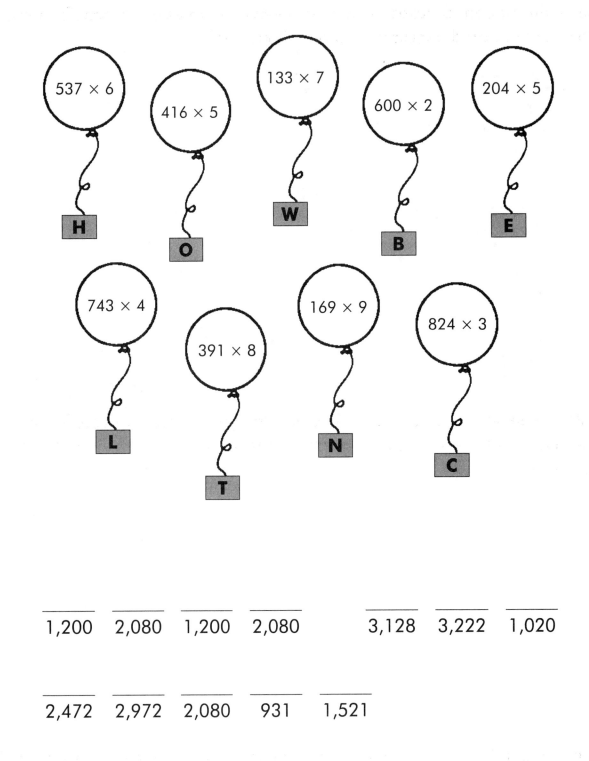

1,200   2,080   1,200   2,080   3,128   3,222   1,020

2,472   2,972   2,080   931   1,521

Solve the following word problems. Show your work in the space below.

62

Singapore Math Practice Level 3A

19. Demetrius bought 6 boxes of colored pencils. There were 15 pencils in each box. How many colored pencils were there altogether?

20. 230 people went to a concert on Friday. If the daily number of people who went to the concert over the next 2 days was the same, what was the total number of people who went to the concert?

21. Sam bought 3 television sets at an electronics store. Each television set cost $637.

How much did he spend at the electronics store?

22. Brittany bought 5 bottles of syrup at a supermarket. Each bottle contained 750 mL of syrup. Find the total volume of syrup that Brittany bought.

23. There were 153 cars in a parking lot. Each car had 4 wheels. How many wheels were there altogether?

REVIEW 3

Look at the pictures carefully. Fill in each blank with the correct answer.

1.

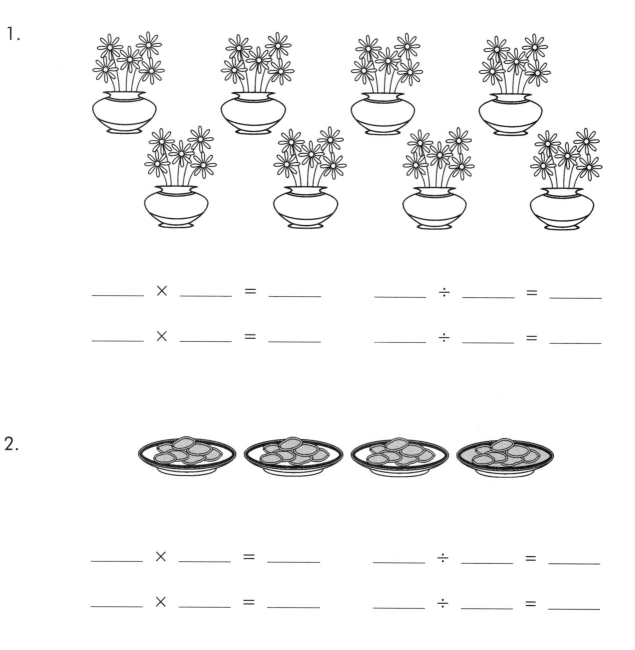

_____ × _____ = _____   _____ ÷ _____ = _____

_____ × _____ = _____   _____ ÷ _____ = _____

2.

_____ × _____ = _____   _____ ÷ _____ = _____

_____ × _____ = _____   _____ ÷ _____ = _____

Solve the following multiplication problems. Show your work.

3.
```
    1 4 7
  ×     8
  _____
```

5.
```
    6 3 2
  ×     4
  _____
```

4.
```
    3 1 2
  ×     3
  _____
```

6.
```
    5 0 0
  ×     3
  _____
```

Study the pictures carefully. Fill in each blank with the correct answer.

7.

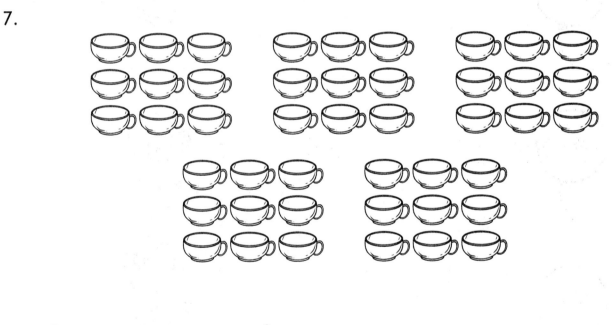

There are _____ groups of mugs.

There are _____ mugs in each group.

There are _____ mugs altogether.

Singapore Math Practice Level 3A

Match each balloon to the correct girl.

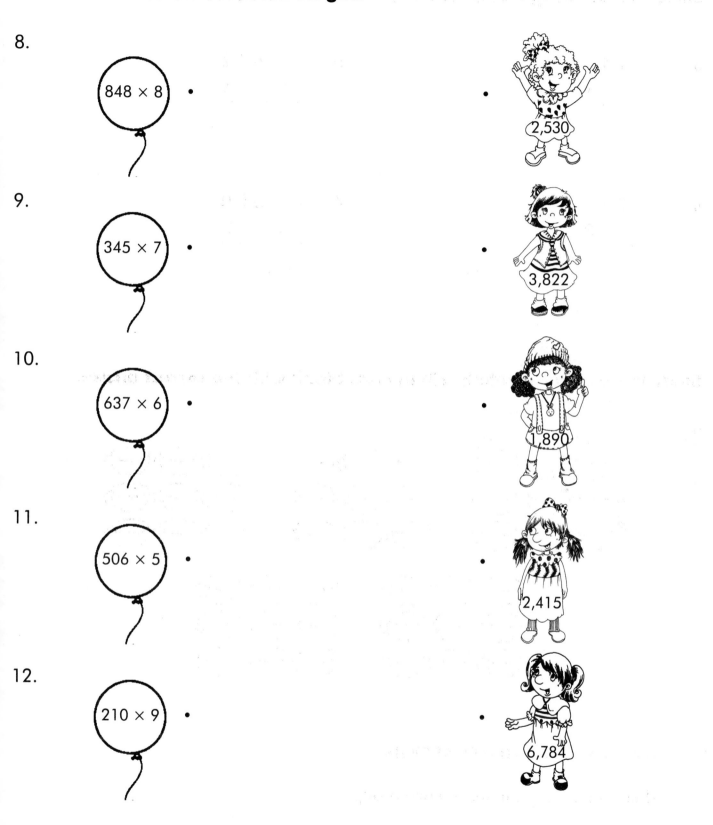

8.

848 × 8

2,530

9.

345 × 7

3,822

10.

637 × 6

1,890

11.

506 × 5

2,415

12.

210 × 9

6,784

Fill in each blank with the correct answer.

13. 9 sixes = _____

14. _____ × 8 = 56

15. 4 × _____ = 28

16. _____ × 9 = 63

Solve the following word problems. Show your work in the space below.

17. Maddy uses 139 beads to make a bag. How many beads does she need to make 8 bags?

Singapore Math Practice Level 3A

18. Vijay has 235 stamps in an album. He has 7 albums in his collection. How many stamps does he have altogether?

19. Ava bought 9 packets of ribbons. If there were 54 ribbons in all, how many ribbons were there in each packet?

20. If a car can transport 5 people, how many people can 45 cars transport?

Unit 7: DIVIDING NUMBERS

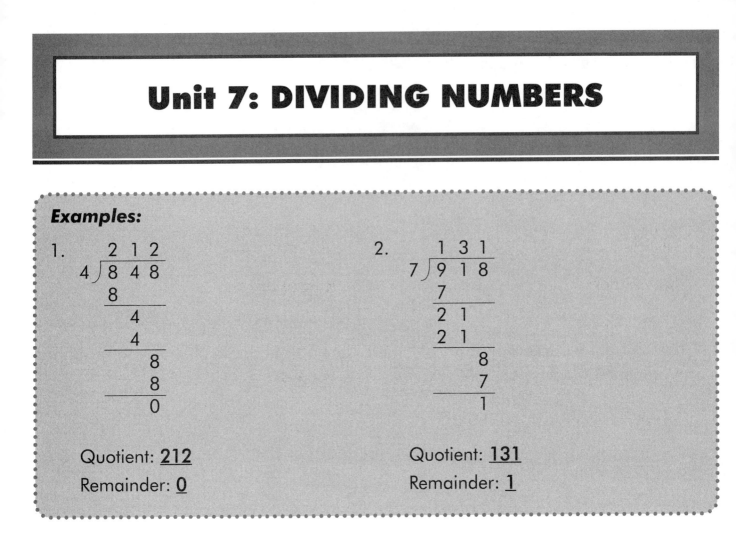

Examples:

1.
```
      2 1 2
  4 ) 8 4 8
      8
      ─────
        4
        4
      ─────
          8
          8
      ─────
          0
```

Quotient: **212**

Remainder: **0**

2.
```
      1 3 1
  7 ) 9 1 8
      7
      ─────
      2 1
      2 1
      ─────
            8
            7
      ─────
            1
```

Quotient: **131**

Remainder: **1**

Solve the following division problems. Show your work.

1. 7) 6 7

2. 5) 1 7

Quotient: _____

Remainder: _____

Quotient: _____

Remainder: _____

Singapore Math Practice Level 3A

3. $3\overline{)25}$

Quotient: _____

Remainder: _____

6. $6\overline{)52}$

Quotient: _____

Remainder: _____

4. $9\overline{)88}$

Quotient: _____

Remainder: _____

7. $2\overline{)469}$

Quotient: _____

Remainder: _____

5. $4\overline{)29}$

Quotient: _____

Remainder: _____

8. $5\overline{)90}$

Quotient: _____

9. $3\overline{)84}$

12. $6\overline{)138}$

Quotient: _____

10. 8)‾7‾9‾2‾

Quotient: _____

11. 7)‾6‾3‾7‾

Quotient: _____

15. 4)‾8‾1‾2‾

Quotient: _____

13. 3)‾7‾0‾2‾

Quotient: _____

14. 9)‾9‾7‾2‾

Singapore Math Practice Level 3A

Quotient: _____

16. Bryan is buying a birthday present for his brother. Solve the division problems to find out what the present is.

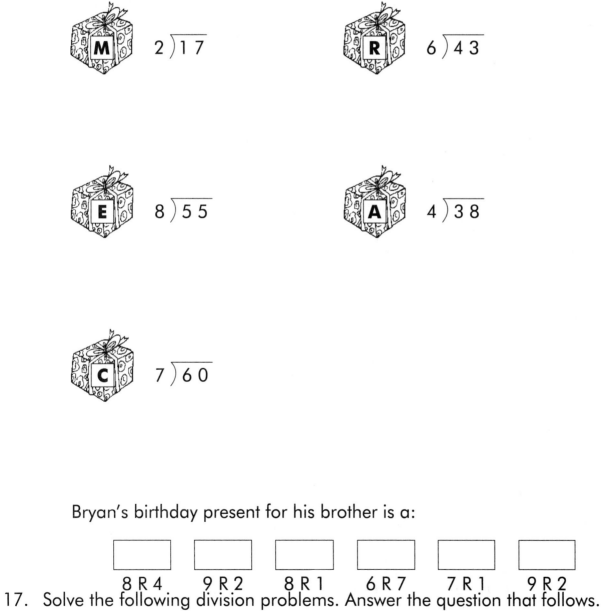

M   2)17   R   6)43

E   8)55   A   4)38

C   7)60

Bryan's birthday present for his brother is a:

8 R 4	9 R 2	8 R 1	6 R 7	7 R 1	9 R 2

17. Solve the following division problems. Answer the question that follows.

Singapore Math Practice Level 3A

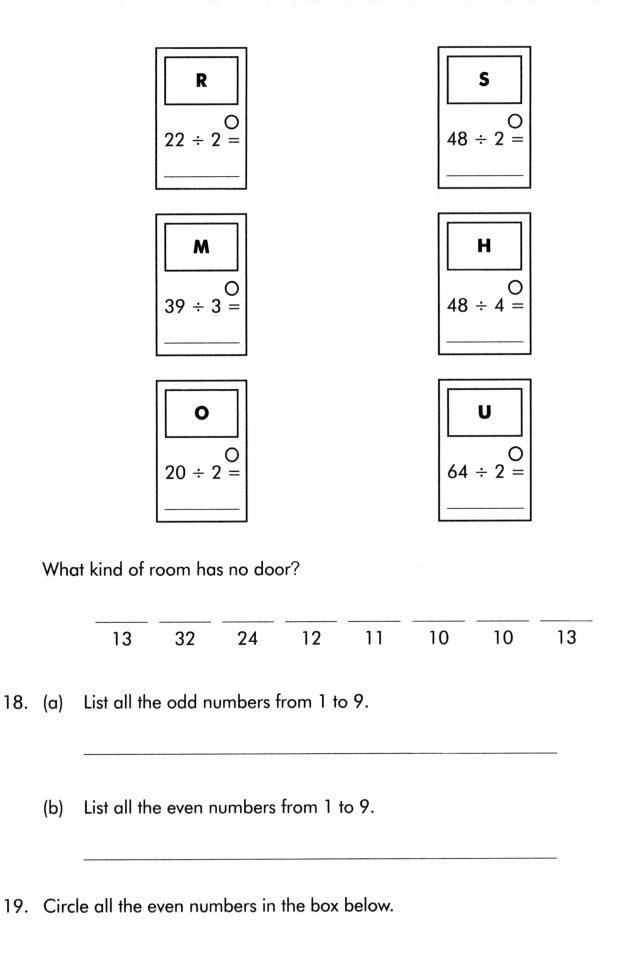

R	S
$22 \div 2 =$ ○	$48 \div 2 =$ ○

M	H
$39 \div 3 =$ ○	$48 \div 4 =$ ○

O	U
$20 \div 2 =$ ○	$64 \div 2 =$ ○

What kind of room has no door?

___ ___ ___ ___ ___ ___ ___ ___
13   32   24   12   11   10   10   13

18. (a) List all the odd numbers from 1 to 9.

_____

(b) List all the even numbers from 1 to 9.

_____

19. Circle all the even numbers in the box below.

Singapore Math Practice Level 3A

33	48	56	97	45
16	74	82	20	

20. Cross out all the odd numbers in the box below.

11	8	65	83	37
20	49	7	91	52

21. What is the largest even number you can make using the digits 3, 0, 9, and 7?

_____

22. What is the smallest odd number you can make using the digits 4, 1, 5, and 2?

_____

Solve the following word problems. Show your work in the space below.

23. John bought 6 boxes of paperclips. He had 426 paperclips altogether. How many paperclips were there in each box?

24. A car manufacturer used 958 tires in June. If each car used 4 tires, how many cars

did he manufacture in June?

25. Beatriz bakes 167 mini muffins. She gives all the muffins to her students. Each student gets 5 mini muffins.

(a) How many students does she have in her class?

(b) How many muffins does she have left?

Unit 8: PROBLEM SOLVING (MULTIPLYING AND DIVIDING)

Examples:

1. Mike saves $650 every month.

   (a) How much will he save in 9 months?

   (b) If he uses $962 to purchase a computer after 9 months, how much will he have left?

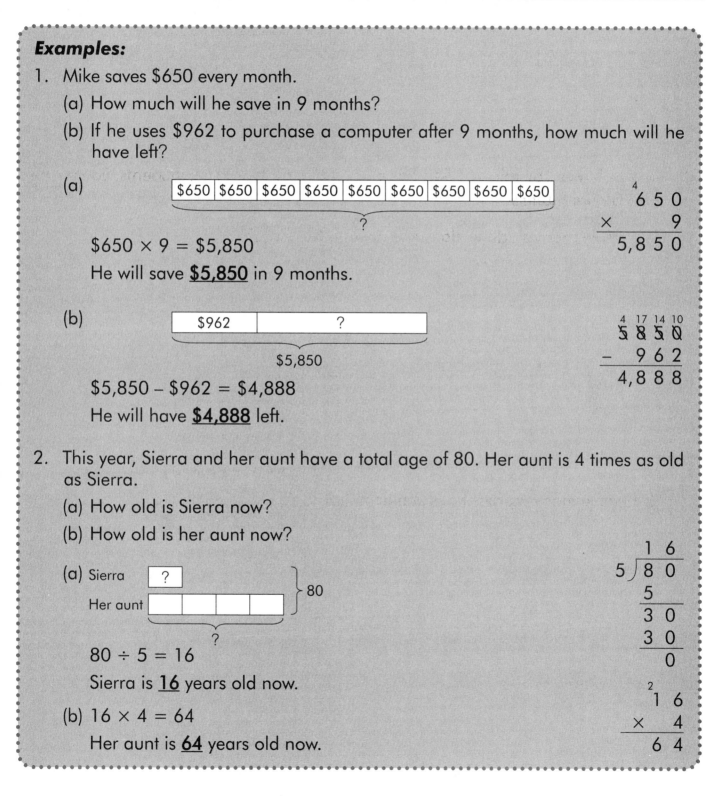

   (a)

   $650 × 9 = $5,850

   He will save **$5,850** in 9 months.

   $$\begin{array}{r} ^4\ \ \ \\ 6\ 5\ 0 \\ \times\quad 9 \\ \hline 5,8\ 5\ 0 \end{array}$$

   (b)

   $5,850 – $962 = $4,888

   He will have **$4,888** left.

   $$\begin{array}{r} ^{4\ \ 17\ 14\ 10}\\ 5\ 8\ 5\ 0 \\ -\quad 9\ 6\ 2 \\ \hline 4,8\ 8\ 8 \end{array}$$

2. This year, Sierra and her aunt have a total age of 80. Her aunt is 4 times as old as Sierra.

   (a) How old is Sierra now?

   (b) How old is her aunt now?

   (a) Sierra

   $80 ÷ 5 = 16$

   Sierra is **16** years old now.

   $$\begin{array}{r} 1\ 6 \\ 5\overline{)8\ 0} \\ 5 \\ \hline 3\ 0 \\ 3\ 0 \\ \hline 0 \end{array}$$

   (b) 16 × 4 = 64

   Her aunt is **64** years old now.

   $$\begin{array}{r} ^2\ \ \\ 1\ 6 \\ \times\quad 4 \\ \hline 6\ 4 \end{array}$$

77

Singapore Math Practice Level 3A

Solve the following word problems. Show your work in the space below.

1. Linh saved $135 in January. She saved twice as much in March. How much did Linh save in March?

2. Brooke bakes 484 dog biscuits. Annie bakes 4 times as many dog biscuits as Brooke. How many dog biscuits does Annie bake?

3. 187 people watched a movie on Wednesday. 3 times as many people watched the same movie over the weekend. How many people watched the movie that weekend?

4. Bakery A sold 565 loaves of bread. Bakery B sold twice as many loaves of bread as

Singapore Math Practice Level 3A

Bakery A. How many loaves of bread did Bakery B sell?

5. Cooper bought 8 packages of baseball cards. There were 25 cards in each package. How many baseball cards did he buy altogether?

6. Larry owns a fish farm. He bought 1,506 fish to be divided equally among his 3 ponds. How many fish could he put into each pond?

7. Alex spent $516 on transportation over 6 months. He spent an equal amount of

money on transportation every month. How much did Alex spend on transportation each month?

8. Keiko has 679 beads. She uses 8 beads to make a ring.

    (a) How many rings can Keiko make?

    (b) How many beads are left?

9. Hasaan earns $1,375 a month. John earns $70 less than Hasaan. Luis earns twice

as much as John.

(a) How much does John earn?

(b) How much does Luis earn?

10. There are 425 girls in a school. There are twice as many boys as girls.

(a) How many boys are there?

(b) How many students are there altogether?

Singapore Math Practice Level 3A

11. Sean collected 312 stamps last month. He collected 68 more stamps this month.

    (a) How many stamps did Sean collect this month?

    (b) How many stamps would each friend get if Sean's collection for this month was shared equally between his 2 friends?

12. Lauren spends $175 on food every month. Jade spends $159 on food every month.

(a) How much more money does Lauren spend on food than Jade?

(b) How much more money does Lauren spend on food than Jade in 6 months?

13. Mr. McKay travels 98 km from his home to the city. He travels the same distance back home.

(a) How far does Mr. McKay travel to and from the city?

(b) Mr. McKay has to travel to and from the city every day in a week. How far will he travel in all?

Singapore Math Practice Level 3A

14. Emelda saved $160 every month for half a year. She then bought 8 presents with the money she saved.

    (a) How much did Emelda save in half a year?

    (b) What was the cost of each present if Emelda paid the same amount of money for all the presents?

15. Audrey sews 8 dresses in a week. Each dress uses 6 yd. of fabric.

    (a) How much fabric does she use in a week?

(b) If she buys 100 yd. of fabric, how much fabric does she have left?

16. Kelly bought 9 packages of crayons. There were 25 crayons in each package. If Kelly were to give 5 crayons to each student, how many students did she have?

17. Kyra bought 3 crates of apples. There were 24 apples in each crate. She then bought 245 oranges. How many pieces of fruit did she buy altogether?

Singapore Math Practice Level 3A

18. A radio costs $95. A television set costs $190. If Ken buys 2 radios and a television set, how much money does he need?

19. Charley bought a chair for $75. He then bought a table that cost 3 times as much as the chair. How much did Charley pay for the furniture?

Singapore Math Practice Level 3A

20. Maria scored a total of 171 points in English and math. She scored twice as many points in English as she did in math. How many points did she score in English?

Unit 9: MENTAL CALCULATIONS

Examples:

1. Add 75 and 21 mentally.

    Step 1: 21 = 2 tens 1 one

    Step 2: 75 + 20 = 95

    Step 3: 95 + 1 = 96

    75 + 21 = **96**

3. Subtract 26 from 67 mentally.

    Step 1: 26 = 2 tens 6 ones

    Step 2: 67 − 20 = 47

    Step 3: 47 − 6 = 41

    67 − 26 = **41**

2. Add 59 and 38 mentally.

    Step 1: 60 = 59 + 1

    Step 2: 60 + 38 = 98

    Step 3: 98 − 1 = 97

    59 + 38 = **97**

4. Subtract 48 from 81 mentally.

    Step 1: 50 = 48 + 2

    Step 2: 81 − 50 = 31

    Step 3: 31 + 2 = 33

    81 − 48 = **33**

5. Find 6 × 90.

    6 × 90 = 6 × 9 tens = 54 tens = **540**

6. Find 4,900 ÷ 7.

    4,900 ÷ 7 = 49 hundreds ÷ 7 = 7 hundreds = **700**

Singapore Math Practice Level 3A

Solve the following problems.

1. $65 + 24 =$ _____

2. $39 + 13 =$ _____

3. $56 + 78 =$ _____

4. $84 + 44 =$ _____

5. $74 + 25 =$ _____

6. $31 + 87 =$ _____

7. $42 + 48 =$ _____

8. $61 + 97 =$ _____

9. $57 + 29 =$ _____

10. $19 + 58 =$ _____

11. $49 - 18 =$ _____

12. $74 - 53 =$ _____

13. $64 - 19 =$ _____

14. $83 - 28 =$ _____

15. $37 - 9 =$ _____

16. $86 - 47 =$ _____

17. $62 - 35 =$ _____

18. $77 - 46 =$ _____

19. $96 - 47 =$ _____

20. $55 - 27 =$ _____

Singapore Math Practice Level 3A

21. $5 \times 8 =$ _____

22. $9 \times 9 =$ _____

23. $7 \times 3 =$ _____

24. $3 \times 6 =$ _____

25. $4 \times 7 =$ _____

26. $2 \times 9 =$ _____

27. $8 \times 60 =$ _____

28. $6 \times 70 =$ _____

29. $3 \times 400 =$ _____

30. $5 \times 500 =$ _____

31. $24 \div 3 =$ _____

32. $54 \div 6 =$ _____

33. $50 \div 5 =$ _____

34. $72 \div 8 =$ _____

35. $90 \div 9 =$ _____

36. $80 \div 4 =$ _____

37. $350 \div 7 =$ _____

38. $210 \div 3 =$ _____

39. $360 \div 6 =$ _____

40. $160 \div 4 =$ _____

Solve the following division problems. Show your work.

1. $7\overline{)537}$

    Quotient: _____

    Remainder: _____

3. $9\overline{)908}$

    Quotient: _____

    Remainder: _____

2. $6\overline{)612}$

    Quotient: _____

4. $4\overline{)504}$

    Quotient: _____

5. What is the smallest 4-digit even number you can make using the digits 3, 5, 2, and 8?

    _____

6. What is the largest 4-digit odd number you can make using the digits 4, 8, 9, and 3.

    _____

Singapore Math Practice Level 3A

7. Solve the following problems to find out where Joseph is going.

　　（I）$7\overline{)357}$　　　　　　（R）$4\overline{)824}$

　　（B）$3\overline{)954}$　　　　　　（A）$5\overline{)675}$

　　（Y）$6\overline{)714}$　　　　　　（L）$9\overline{)711}$　60
　　　　　　　　　　　　　　　　　　　　　450
　　　　　　　　　　　　　　　　　　　　　$\overline{261}$

___	___	___	___	___	___	___
79	51	318	206	135	206	119

8. Find the quotient when 278 is divided by 2.　　　　_____

9. Add 37 and 69 mentally.　　　　_____

10. List all the odd numbers from 50 to 60.

_____

11. Subtract 19 from 34 mentally.　　　　_____

12. Find the quotient when 400 is divided by 8.　　　　_____

Singapore Math Practice Level 3A

13. List all the even numbers from 30 to 40.

_____

14. Find the product of 8 and 5 mentally.   _____

15. Find the quotient when 24 is divided by 6.   _____

Solve the following word problems. Show your work in the space below.

16. Serena buys 4 bags of noodles. There are 5 packets of noodles in each bag.

    (a) How many packets of noodles are there altogether?

    (b) Serena gives all the packets of noodles to her friends. If each of her friends
         receives 2 packets of noodles, how many friends does she give the noodles to?

17. Rashid has 6 albums of stamps. There are 230 stamps in each album. He gives the

Singapore Math Practice Level 3A

stamps to his 3 nephews. How many stamps does each nephew receive?

18. Anya uses 8 packets of sugar to bake 2 loaves of banana bread. Each packet of sugar has a mass of 50 g. How much sugar does she need for each loaf of banana bread?

19. Shop A sells 3 toys for $27. Shop B sells the same toys at 5 for $40. If Sadie wants

to buy only 1 toy, which shop sells the toy at a cheaper price?

20. Nick travels a total of 464 yd. from his house to the city and back to his house.

(a) How far is Nick's house from the city?

(b) How far would Nick travel in 5 days if he were to travel from his house to the city and back to his house?

Singapore Math Practice Level 3A

FINAL REVIEW

Write the numbers on the lines.

1. seven thousand, three hundred   _____

2. four thousand, forty   _____

Write the following numbers as words on the lines.

3. 5,015   _____

4. 6,411   _____

Write the correct answers on the lines.

5. Find the sum of 3,618 and 2,934.   _____

6. Find the difference between 4,372 and 2,465.   _____

7. Multiply 149 by 7.   _____

8. Find the remainder when 863 is divided by 8.   _____

9. Add 16 and 25 mentally.   _____

Singapore Math Practice Level 3A

Solve the following problems. Show your work.

10.   3,8 9 1
      + 4,6 2 3
      _____

13.   8,2 3 0
      − 1,9 6 5
      _____

11.   9,0 0 0
      − 4,5 1 5
      _____

14.   4 1 4
      ×   8
      _____

12. 7$\overline{)800}$

15. 4$\overline{)312}$

16. Arrange these numbers in order. Begin with the smallest.

6,302, 4,263, 8,143, 2,436

_____, _____, _____, _____

17. Fill in the blank with *greater* or *smaller*.

5,920 is _____ than 5,820.

18. Look at the picture carefully. Write 2 multiplication and division sentences.

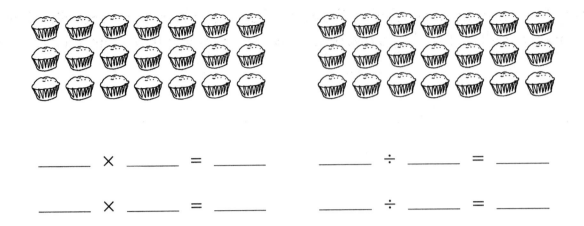

_____ × _____ = _____   _____ ÷ _____ = _____

_____ × _____ = _____   _____ ÷ _____ = _____

19. Complete the number pattern.

2,017, _____, _____, 2,317, 2,417

20.

There are _____ groups of baskets.

There are _____ baskets in each group.

There are _____ baskets altogether.

Singapore Math Practice Level 3A

Solve the following word problems. Show your work in the space below.

21. Rachel has 8 bags of seashells. There are 55 seashells in each bag. She then packs all the seashells into 2 bags equally. How many seashells are there in each bag?

22. Carson has 316 bottle caps. James has 3 times as many bottle caps as Carson. Dan has 400 fewer bottle caps than James. How many bottle caps does Dan have?

Singapore Math Practice Level 3A

23. Amrita walks 1,416 yd. to the library from her house. She then goes to a shop which is 165 yd. from the library.

(a) How far is the shop from her house?

(b) Amrita walks to the library and to the shop from her house, using the same route home. How far does she walk?

24. The distance from Kovan City to Lakeview City is 138 km. There are 3 bus stops of equal distance between the 2 cities. If Olivia boards the bus at the first bus stop and gets off at the second bus stop, how far will she travel?

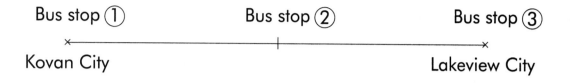

25. Monica paid $1,450 for a sofa. She paid twice as much for an entertainment center. If she gave the cashier $5,000, how much change would she receive?

Singapore Math Practice Level 3A

CHALLENGE QUESTIONS

Solve the following problems on another sheet of paper.

1. The chart below shows the amount of money Simon saves from Monday to Wednesday.

Monday	Tuesday	Wednesday
$6	$12	$18

    If Simon continues to save in this pattern, how much money will he save by Sunday?

2. Complete the number pattern.

    3, 4, 7, 11, 18, 29, 47, _____, _____, _____

3. At a party, 6 handshakes were exchanged. Assuming that each person shook hands with another person once, how many people were at the party?

4. Form 2-digit numbers with the digits 1, 2, and 3. The digits in each number cannot be repeated. List all the 2-digit numbers that can be divided by 4.

5. Number X is a 4-digit even number. All its digits are different. The largest digit is in the tens place, and the smallest digit is in the hundreds place. The sum of the first 2 digits is 8 less than the sum of the last 2 digits. The sum of all its digits is 26. What is Number X if it is less than 6,000?

6. I am a number between 20 and 39. If I am divided by 5, there will be a remainder of 2. If I am divided by 6, there will be a remainder of 2. What number am I?

7. Complete the number pattern.

    2, 6, 10, 15, 20, 24, _____, _____, 38, 42, _____, _____

Singapore Math Practice Level 3A

8. A group of 6 people shook hands with one another in a meeting. Each person shook hands with another person once. How many handshakes were exchanged?

9. When a bag of peaches is shared among 3 boys, there is 1 peach left. When the bag of peaches is shared among 4 boys, there is 1 peach left. How many peaches are there in the bag? (Assume that the number of peaches is not greater than 20.)

10. The first digit of a number is the same as the last digit. The second digit is 1 more than the first digit. The sum of all its digits is 4. Find the 3-digit odd number.

11. The chart below shows the number of workers and the number of days needed to build a 2-story building. Find the number of days needed for 10 workers to build the same building.

Number of workers	Number of days needed
50	32
40	44
30	56
20	68
10	?

12. When a book of 100 pages is opened, the sum of the facing page numbers can be divided by 5. The quotient is a product of 3 and 7. What are the facing page numbers?

Unit 1: Numbers 1–10,000

1. **3,625**
2. **9,099**
3. **6,208**
4. **5,817**
5. **8,035**
6. **nine thousand, six hundred ninety-three**
7. **four thousand, three hundred thirteen**
8. **eight thousand, four hundred forty**
9. **seven thousand, fifteen**
10. **six thousand, five hundred five**
11. **8,070, 8,090**
    8,060 – 8,050 = 10
    8,060 + 10 = 8,070
    8,080 + 10 = 8,090
12. **2,211, 2,411**
    2,111 + 100 = 2,211
    2,311 + 100 = 2,411
13. **5,593, 7,593**
    4,593 – 3,593 = 1,000
    4,593 + 1,000 = 5,593
    6,593 + 1,000 = 7,593
14. **2099, 2399**
    2,299 – 2,199 = 100
    1,999 + 100 = 2,099
    2,299 + 100 = 2,399
15. **7,090, 7,110**
    7,080 + 10 = 7,090
    7,100 + 10 = 7,110
16. **3, 7, 4, 0**
17. **9, 3, 6, 1**
18. **7, 0, 0, 1**
19. **6,000, 300, 80, 4**
20. **1,000, 0, 70, 2**
21. **4,000, 900, 50, 1**
22. **800**
23. **2,000**
24. **600**
25. (a) **0**
    (b) **thousands**
    (c) **500**
    (d) **4**
26. (a) **4**
    (b) **ones**
    (c) **20**
    (d) **8**
27. (a) **5**
    (b) **tens**
    (c) **700**

(d) **1**
28. **6,447**
29. **1,047**
30. **4,196**
31. **6,656**
32. **8,942**
33. **3,010**
34. **4,614**
35. **9,999**
36. **5,551**
37. **2,468**
38. **3,829**
39. **2,056**
40. **smaller**
41. **greater**
42. **greater**
43. **greater**
44. **smaller**
45. **1,550, 1,555**
    1,545 – 1,540 = 5
    1,545 + 5 = 1,550
    1,550 + 5 = 1,555
46. **4,769, 4,469**
    4,669 – 4,569 = 100
    4,869 – 100 = 4,769
    4,569 – 100 = 4,469
47. **2,350, 2,370**
    2,340 – 2,330 = 10
    2,340 + 10 = 2,350
    2,360 + 10 = 2,370
48. **7,719, 6,719**
    5,719 – 4,719 = 1,000
    8,719 – 1,000 = 7,719
    7,719 – 1,000 = 6,719
49. **5,896, 5,906**
    5,886 – 5,876 = 10
    5,886 + 10 = 5,896
    5,896 + 10 = 5,906
50. **9,316, 6,193, 3,619, 1,936**
51. **5,850, 5,805, 5,508, 5,058**
52. **9,963, 9,396, 6,939, 3,699**
53. **4,210, 4,120, 2,104, 2,014**
54. **8,616, 8,116, 6,881, 6,818**
55. **1,424, 2,424, 4,424, 8,424**
56. **8,001, 8,011, 8,101, 8,118**
57. **4,025, 4,520, 5,045, 5,240**
58. **3,369, 3,693, 6,339, 6,933**
59. **4,169, 4,619, 4,691, 4,916**
60. **8,621**
61. **3,579**

Unit 2: Adding Numbers up to 10,000

1. $1,386 + 2,001 =$ **3,387**

$$\begin{array}{r} 1,3\,8\,6 \\ +\ 2,0\,0\,1 \\ \hline 3,3\,8\,7 \end{array}$$

2. $5,210 + 4,689 =$ **9,899**

$$\begin{array}{r} 5,2\,1\,0 \\ +\ 4,6\,8\,9 \\ \hline 9,8\,9\,9 \end{array}$$

3. $4,037 + 2,232 =$ **6,269**

$$\begin{array}{r} 4,0\,3\,7 \\ +\ 2,2\,3\,2 \\ \hline 6,2\,6\,9 \end{array}$$

4. $6,512 + 3,076 =$ **9,588**

$$\begin{array}{r} 6,5\,1\,2 \\ +\ 3,0\,7\,6 \\ \hline 9,5\,8\,8 \end{array}$$

5. $4,378 + 1,521 =$ **5,899**

$$\begin{array}{r} 4,3\,7\,8 \\ +\ 1,5\,2\,1 \\ \hline 5,8\,9\,9 \end{array}$$

6. **11, 9**
    1, 1, 9
    3 hundreds 6 tens + 8 hundreds 3 tens
    = 3 + 8 hundreds 6 + 3 tens
    = 11 hundreds 9 tens
    = 1 thousand 1 hundred 9 tens

7. **11, 13, 5**
    1, 2, 3, 5
    5 hundreds 9 tens 3 ones + 6 hundreds 4 tens 2 ones
    = 5 + 6 hundreds 9 + 4 tens 3 + 2 ones
    = 11 hundreds 13 tens 5 ones
    = 1 thousand 2 hundreds 3 tens 5 ones

8. **12, 8, 13**
    1, 2, 9, 3
    7 hundreds 6 tens 9 ones + 5 hundreds 2 tens 4 ones
    = 7 + 5 hundreds 6 + 2 tens 9 + 4 ones
    = 12 hundreds 8 tens 13 ones
    = 1 thousand 2 hundreds 9 tens 3 ones

9. **12, 10, 14**
    1, 3, 1, 4
    4 hundreds 2 tens 5 ones + 8 hundreds 8 tens 9 ones
    = 4 + 8 hundreds 2 + 8 tens 5 + 9 ones
    = 12 hundreds 10 tens 14 ones
    = 1 thousand 3 hundreds 1 ten 4 ones

10. **17, 6, 5**
    1, 7, 6, 5
    9 hundreds 1 ten 5 ones + 8 hundreds 5 tens
    = 9 + 8 hundreds 1 + 5 tens 5 ones
    = 17 hundreds 6 tens 5 ones
    = 1 thousand 7 hundreds 6 tens 5 ones

11. $2,790 + 5,637 =$ **8,427**

$$\begin{array}{r} 2,7\,9\,0 \\ +\ 5,6\,3\,7 \\ \hline 8,4\,2\,7 \end{array}$$

12. $4,078 + 3,659 =$ **7,737**

$$\begin{array}{r} 4,0\,7\,8 \\ +\ 3,6\,5\,9 \\ \hline 7,7\,3\,7 \end{array}$$

13. $8,316 + 1,473 =$ **9,789**

$$\begin{array}{r} 8,3\,1\,6 \\ +\ 1,4\,7\,3 \\ \hline 9,7\,8\,9 \end{array}$$

14.
$$\begin{array}{r} 1,7\,4\,5 \\ +\ 6,4\,8\,7 \\ \hline \mathbf{8,2\,3\,2} \end{array}$$

15.
$$\begin{array}{r} 8,4\,0\,0 \\ +\ 1,3\,2\,4 \\ \hline \mathbf{9,7\,2\,4} \end{array}$$

16.
$$\begin{array}{r} 3,3\,5\,6 \\ +\ 4,1\,3\,4 \\ \hline \mathbf{7,4\,9\,0} \end{array}$$

17.
$$\begin{array}{r} 4,3\,4\,8 \\ +\ 1,6\,2\,5 \\ \hline \mathbf{5,9\,7\,3} \end{array}$$

18.
$$\begin{array}{r} 7,4\,3\,0 \\ +\ 1,9\,3\,2 \\ \hline \mathbf{9,3\,6\,2} \end{array}$$

19.
$$\begin{array}{r} 2,2\,8\,2 \\ +\ 5,4\,1\,3 \\ \hline \mathbf{7,6\,9\,5} \end{array}$$

20.
$$\begin{array}{r} 4,9\,0\,8 \\ +\ 1,7\,6\,7 \\ \hline \mathbf{6,6\,7\,5} \end{array}$$

21.
$$\begin{array}{r} 6,2\,1\,0 \\ +\ 1,5\,3\,8 \\ \hline \mathbf{7,7\,4\,8} \end{array}$$

22.
$$\begin{array}{r} 9,1\,2\,6 \\ +\ \ \ \ 1\,4\,2 \\ \hline \mathbf{9,2\,6\,8} \end{array}$$

23.
$$\begin{array}{r} 4,8\,1\,3 \\ +\ 4,1\,3\,5 \\ \hline \mathbf{8,9\,4\,8} \end{array}$$

24.
$$\begin{array}{r} 5,4\,1\,0 \\ +\ 2,3\,8\,5 \\ \hline \mathbf{7,7\,9\,5} \end{array}$$

25.
$$\begin{array}{r} 3,8\,6\,9 \\ +\ 2,4\,3\,5 \\ \hline \mathbf{6,3\,0\,4} \end{array}$$

26.
$$\begin{array}{r} 3,8\,6\,3 \\ +\ 5,5\,7\,6 \\ \hline \mathbf{9,4\,3\,9} \end{array}$$

27.
$$\begin{array}{r} 5,6\,5\,7 \\ +\ 3,6\,3\,8 \\ \hline \mathbf{9,2\,9\,5} \end{array}$$

28.
$$\begin{array}{r} 5,3\,7\,5 \\ +\ 2,9\,1\,7 \\ \hline \mathbf{8,2\,9\,2} \end{array}$$

29.
$$\begin{array}{r} 6,2\,8\,1 \\ +\ 1,1\,9\,8 \\ \hline \mathbf{7,4\,7\,9} \end{array}$$

30.
$$\begin{array}{r} 4,6\,3\,3 \\ +\ 3,0\,4\,7 \\ \hline \mathbf{7,6\,8\,0} \end{array}$$

31.
$$\begin{array}{r} 2,2\,8\,2 \\ +\ 4,0\,6\,0 \\ \hline \mathbf{6,3\,4\,2} \end{array}$$

Singapore Math Practice Level 3A

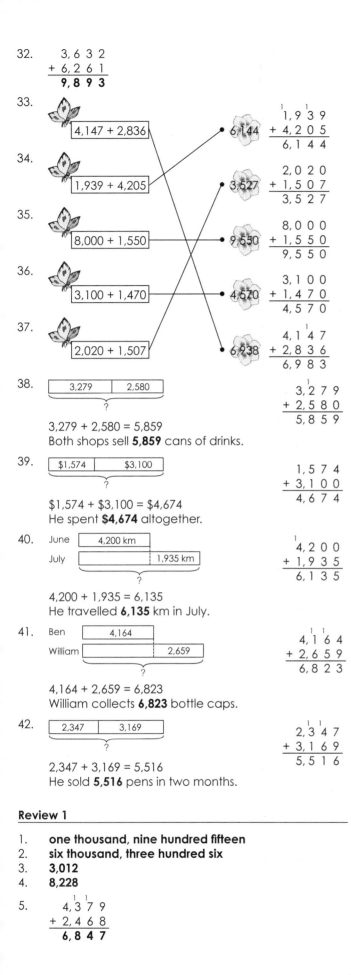

32.
```
   3,6 3 2
 + 6,2 6 1
   9,8 9 3
```

33. 4,147 + 2,836

34. 1,939 + 4,205

35. 8,000 + 1,550

36. 3,100 + 1,470

37. 2,020 + 1,507

6,144
```
   1,9 3 9
 + 4,2 0 5
   6,1 4 4
```

3,527
```
   2,0 2 0
 + 1,5 0 7
   3,5 2 7
```

9,550
```
   8,0 0 0
 + 1,5 5 0
   9,5 5 0
```

4,570
```
   3,1 0 0
 + 1,4 7 0
   4,5 7 0
```

6,938
```
   4,1 4 7
 + 2,8 3 6
   6,9 8 3
```

38.
| 3,279 | 2,580 |
?

```
   3,2 7 9
 + 2,5 8 0
   5,8 5 9
```
3,279 + 2,580 = 5,859
Both shops sell **5,859** cans of drinks.

39.
| $1,574 | $3,100 |
?

```
   1,5 7 4
 + 3,1 0 0
   4,6 7 4
```
$1,574 + $3,100 = $4,674
He spent **$4,674** altogether.

40.
June 4,200 km
July 1,935 km
?

```
   4,2 0 0
 + 1,9 3 5
   6,1 3 5
```
4,200 + 1,935 = 6,135
He travelled **6,135** km in July.

41.
Ben 4,164
William 2,659
?

```
   4,1 6 4
 + 2,6 5 9
   6,8 2 3
```
4,164 + 2,659 = 6,823
William collects **6,823** bottle caps.

42.
| 2,347 | 3,169 |
?

```
   2,3 4 7
 + 3,1 6 9
   5,5 1 6
```
2,347 + 3,169 = 5,516
He sold **5,516** pens in two months.

Review 1

1. **one thousand, nine hundred fifteen**
2. **six thousand, three hundred six**
3. **3,012**
4. **8,228**
5.
```
   4,3 7 9
 + 2,4 6 8
   6,8 4 7
```

6.
```
   1,0 0 2
 + 2,8 9 9
   3,9 0 1
```

7.
```
   5,3 8 5
 + 2,4 1 8
   7,8 0 3
```

8.
```
   4,0 1 6
 + 3,8 4 9
   7,8 6 5
```

9. **4,798**
10. **1,050**
11. **3,717**
12. **6,203**
13. **4,634, 4,644**
   4,624 – 4,614 = 10
   4,624 + 10 = 4,634
   4,634 + 10 = 4,644
14. **7,918, 7,975**
   7,956 – 7,937 = 19
   7,899 + 19 = 7,918
   7,956 + 19 = 7,975
15. **4,680, 4,860, 6,048, 6,840**
16. (a) **2**
    (b) **6**
    (c) **hundreds**
    (d) **3**
17. 7,096 + 1,845 = **8,941**
```
   7,0 9 6
 + 1,8 4 5
   8,9 4 1
```
18. **13, 4, 9**
    1, 3, 4, 9
    4 + 9 hundreds 3 + 1 tens 4 + 5 ones
    = 13 hundreds 4 tens 9 ones
    = 1 thousand 3 hundreds 4 tens 9 ones
19.
March $4,312
April $688
?

```
   4,3 1 2
 +   6 8 8
   5,0 0 0
```
$4,312 + $688 = $5,000
He saved **$5,000** in April.

20.
bracelet $1,375
necklace $1,999
?

```
   1,3 7 5
 + 1,9 9 9
   3,3 7 4
```
$1,375 + $1,999 = $3,374
Mandy pays **$3,374** for the diamond necklace.

Unit 3: Subtracting Numbers up to 10,000

1. 67 – 17 = **50**
```
   6 7
 - 1 7
   5 0
```

2. 53 – 12 = **41**
```
   5 3
 - 1 2
   4 1
```

3. 548 – 320 = **228**
```
   5 4 8
 - 3 2 0
   2 2 8
```

Singapore Math Practice Level 3A

4.   486 – 35 = **451**

$$\begin{array}{r} 4\,8\,6 \\ -\ \ 3\,5 \\ \hline 4\,5\,1 \end{array}$$

5.   979 – 546 = **433**

$$\begin{array}{r} 9\,7\,9 \\ -5\,4\,6 \\ \hline 4\,3\,3 \end{array}$$

6. $$\begin{array}{r} 3,8\,6\,9 \\ -\ \ 2\,3\,5 \\ \hline \mathbf{3,6\,3\,4} \end{array}$$

7. $$\begin{array}{r} 7,7\,8\,7 \\ -4,3\,2\,5 \\ \hline \mathbf{3,4\,6\,2} \end{array}$$

8. $$\begin{array}{r} 9,\overset{6}{\cancel{7}}\overset{17}{\cancel{7}}6 \\ -1,0\,8\,5 \\ \hline \mathbf{8,6\,9\,1} \end{array}$$

9. $$\begin{array}{r} 5,8\,\overset{7}{\cancel{8}}\overset{11}{\cancel{1}} \\ -4,0\,5\,8 \\ \hline \mathbf{1,8\,2\,3} \end{array}$$

10. $$\begin{array}{r} 2,\overset{8}{\cancel{9}}\overset{10}{\cancel{0}}\,0 \\ -\ \ 8\,9\,0 \\ \hline \mathbf{2,0\,1\,0} \end{array}$$

11. $$\begin{array}{r} 4,1\,\overset{2}{\cancel{3}}\overset{16}{\cancel{6}} \\ -2,1\,2\,8 \\ \hline \mathbf{2,0\,0\,8} \end{array}$$

12. $$\begin{array}{r} 6,8\,4\,8 \\ -2,0\,0\,5 \\ \hline \mathbf{4,8\,4\,3} \end{array}$$

13. $$\begin{array}{r} 2,4\,2\,6 \\ -1,3\,1\,0 \\ \hline \mathbf{1,1\,1\,6} \end{array}$$

14. $$\begin{array}{r} \overset{6}{\cancel{7}},\overset{14}{\cancel{4}}\,3\,1 \\ -5,6\,1\,1 \\ \hline \mathbf{1,8\,2\,0} \end{array}$$

15. $$\begin{array}{r} 8,8\,1\,8 \\ -7,1\,0\,7 \\ \hline \mathbf{1,7\,1\,1} \end{array}$$

16. $$\begin{array}{r} \overset{8}{\cancel{9}},\overset{10}{\cancel{1}}\overset{12}{\cancel{3}}\overset{10}{\cancel{0}} \\ -3,6\,8\,4 \\ \hline \mathbf{5,4\,4\,6} \end{array}$$

17. $$\begin{array}{r} \overset{7}{\cancel{8}},\overset{12}{\cancel{2}}\overset{8}{\cancel{9}}\overset{12}{\cancel{2}} \\ -8,5\,0\,5 \\ \hline \mathbf{5,7\,8\,7} \end{array}$$

18. $$\begin{array}{r} \overset{4}{\cancel{5}},\overset{13}{\cancel{3}}\overset{8}{\cancel{9}}\overset{12}{\cancel{2}} \\ -2,8\,8\,6 \\ \hline \mathbf{2,5\,0\,6} \end{array}$$

19. $$\begin{array}{r} 4,9\,\overset{7}{\cancel{8}}\overset{18}{\cancel{8}} \\ -3,9\,6\,9 \\ \hline \mathbf{1,0\,1\,9} \end{array}$$

20. $$\begin{array}{r} \overset{8}{\cancel{9}},\overset{12}{\cancel{3}}\overset{16}{\cancel{6}}8 \\ -1,4\,8\,7 \\ \hline \mathbf{7,8\,8\,1} \end{array}$$

21. $$\begin{array}{r} \overset{1}{\cancel{2}},\overset{12}{\cancel{3}}\overset{16}{\cancel{7}}\overset{16}{\cancel{6}} \\ -1,4\,8\,7 \\ \hline \mathbf{8\,8\,9} \end{array}$$

22. $$\begin{array}{r} \overset{7}{\cancel{8}},\overset{9}{\cancel{0}}\overset{9}{\cancel{0}}\overset{10}{\cancel{0}} \\ -4,6\,5\,9 \\ \hline \mathbf{3,3\,4\,1} \end{array}$$

23. $$\begin{array}{r} \overset{2}{\cancel{3}},\overset{14}{\cancel{5}}\overset{16}{\cancel{7}}\overset{16}{\cancel{6}} \\ -1,8\,9\,9 \\ \hline \mathbf{1,6\,7\,7} \end{array}$$

24. $$\begin{array}{r} \overset{5}{\cancel{6}},\overset{9}{\cancel{0}}\overset{9}{\cancel{0}}\overset{15}{\cancel{5}} \\ -4,7\,6\,9 \\ \hline \mathbf{1,2\,3\,6} \end{array}$$

25. $$\begin{array}{r} \overset{7}{\cancel{8}},\overset{9}{\cancel{0}}\overset{10}{\cancel{1}}\overset{10}{\cancel{0}} \\ -3,8\,6\,5 \\ \hline \mathbf{4,1\,4\,5} \end{array}$$

26. $$\begin{array}{r} 4,3\,6\,9 \\ -3,1\,2\,4 \\ \hline \mathbf{1,2\,4\,5} \end{array}$$

27. $$\begin{array}{r} 5,1\,3\,9 \\ -2,0\,0\,0 \\ \hline \mathbf{3,1\,3\,9} \end{array}$$

28. $$\begin{array}{r} \overset{4}{\cancel{5}},\overset{13}{\cancel{3}}\overset{4}{\cancel{5}}\overset{13}{\cancel{3}} \\ -1,5\,2\,6 \\ \hline \mathbf{3,8\,2\,7} \end{array}$$

29. $$\begin{array}{r} \overset{2}{\cancel{3}},\overset{12}{\cancel{3}}\overset{14}{\cancel{5}}\overset{10}{\cancel{0}} \\ -1,5\,9\,8 \\ \hline \mathbf{1,7\,5\,2} \end{array}$$

30. $$\begin{array}{r} 6,\overset{1}{\cancel{2}}\overset{10}{\cancel{0}}6 \\ -2,0\,6\,2 \\ \hline \mathbf{4,1\,4\,4} \end{array}$$

31.

G	U	I	T	A	R
1,165	3,489	3,672	2,907	1,655	1,217

$$\begin{array}{r} \overset{2}{\cancel{3}}\overset{9}{\cancel{0}}\overset{13}{\cancel{4}}\overset{10}{\cancel{0}} \\ -1,875 \\ \hline 1,165 \end{array} \quad \begin{array}{r} \overset{7}{\cancel{8}}\overset{9}{\cancel{0}}\overset{9}{\cancel{0}}\overset{18}{\cancel{8}} \\ -4,519 \\ \hline 3,489 \end{array} \quad \begin{array}{r} \overset{5}{\cancel{6}}\overset{15}{\cancel{6}}\overset{16}{\cancel{6}}\overset{}{\cancel{6}} \\ -2,994 \\ \hline 3,672 \end{array} \quad \begin{array}{r} \overset{6}{\cancel{7}}\overset{15}{\cancel{5}}\overset{1}{\cancel{2}}\overset{13}{\cancel{3}} \\ -4,616 \\ \hline 2,907 \end{array} \quad \begin{array}{r} \overset{4}{\cancel{5}}\overset{10}{\cancel{1}}\overset{11}{\cancel{1}}\overset{}{\cancel{5}} \\ -3,460 \\ \hline 1,655 \end{array} \quad \begin{array}{r} \overset{8}{\cancel{4}}\overset{16}{\cancel{8}}\overset{}{\cancel{9}}\overset{}{\cancel{6}} \\ -3,679 \\ \hline 1,217 \end{array}$$

32. Hafiz | 4,376 |
   Alex | ? | } 2,950

$$\begin{array}{r} 4,\overset{3}{\cancel{3}}\overset{13}{\cancel{7}}6 \\ -2,9\,5\,0 \\ \hline 1,4\,2\,6 \end{array}$$

4,376 – 2,950 = 1,426
Alex has **1,426** stickers.

33. necklace | 2,315 |
   bracelet | 1,670 | ?

$$\begin{array}{r} \overset{1}{\cancel{2}},\overset{12}{\cancel{3}}\overset{11}{\cancel{1}}5 \\ -1,6\,7\,0 \\ \hline 6\,4\,5 \end{array}$$

2,315 – 1,670 = 645
She uses **645** fewer beads for the bracelet.

34. June | 5,300 |
   July | ? | 565

$$\begin{array}{r} \overset{4}{\cancel{5}},\overset{12}{\cancel{3}}\overset{9}{\cancel{0}}\overset{10}{\cancel{0}} \\ -\ \ 5\,6\,5 \\ \hline 4,7\,3\,5 \end{array}$$

5,300 – 565 = 4,735
Alicia baked **4,735** muffins in July.

Singapore Math Practice Level 3A

35.

TV | $6,478
laptop | ? | $2,590

$$\begin{array}{r} ^{5}\cancel{6},\overset{13}{\cancel{4}}\overset{17}{\cancel{7}}8 \\ -\ 2,590 \\ \hline 3,888 \end{array}$$

$6,478 − $2,590 = $3,888
The laptop costs **$3,888**.

36.

? | 4,825
9,000

$$\begin{array}{r} ^{8}\overset{9}{\cancel{9}}\overset{9}{\cancel{0}}\overset{10}{\cancel{0}}\cancel{0} \\ -\ 4,825 \\ \hline 4,175 \end{array}$$

9,000 − 4,825 = 4,175
She sold **4,175** stamps on Monday.

Unit 4: Problem Solving (Adding and Subtracting)

1. **(a)**

Mia | 236
Abby | ? | 127

$$\begin{array}{r} 2\overset{2}{\cancel{3}}\overset{16}{\cancel{6}} \\ -\ 127 \\ \hline 109 \end{array}$$

236 − 127 = 109
Abby has **109** stickers.

(b)

236 | 109
?

$$\begin{array}{r} 23\overset{1}{6} \\ +\ 109 \\ \hline 345 \end{array}$$

236 + 109 = 345
They have **345** stickers altogether.

2.

Roberto | 3,280 mi.
Steve | 568 mi.
?

$$\begin{array}{r} 3,2\overset{1}{8}0 \\ +\ \ 568 \\ \hline 3,848 \end{array}$$

3,280 + 568 = 3,848
Steve travels 3,848 m.
3,848 + 3,280 = 7,128
They travel **7,128 mi.** altogether.

$$\begin{array}{r} \overset{1}{3},\overset{1}{8}48 \\ +\ 3,280 \\ \hline 7,128 \end{array}$$

3. **(a)**

Hailey | 2,345
Asia | 3,542

$$\begin{array}{r} 3,\overset{4}{\cancel{5}}\overset{13}{\cancel{4}}\overset{12}{\cancel{2}} \\ -\ 2,345 \\ \hline 1,197 \end{array}$$

3,542 − 2,345 = 1,197
Asia has **1,197** more stamps than Hailey.

(b)

3,542 | 2,345
?

$$\begin{array}{r} 3,542 \\ +\ 2,345 \\ \hline 5,887 \end{array}$$

3,542 + 2,345 = 5,887
They have **5,887** stamps altogether.

4.

Sarah | $2,140
Carmen | $150
Sonya | ? | $270

$$\begin{array}{r} 2,140 \\ +\ \ 150 \\ \hline 2,290 \end{array}$$

$2,140 + $150 = $2,290
$2,290 − $270 = $2,020
Sonya earns **$2,020**.

$$\begin{array}{r} 2,290 \\ -\ \ 270 \\ \hline 2,020 \end{array}$$

5. **(a)**

Rebecca | $2,080
Kimiko | ? | $275

$$\begin{array}{r} \overset{1}{\cancel{2}},\overset{10}{\cancel{0}}\overset{7}{\cancel{8}}\overset{10}{\cancel{0}} \\ -\ \ 275 \\ \hline 1,805 \end{array}$$

$2,080 − $275 = $1,805
Kimiko pays **$1,805** for her television set.

(b)

$2,080 | $1,805
?

$$\begin{array}{r} 2,080 \\ +\ 1,805 \\ \hline 3,885 \end{array}$$

$2,080 + $1,805 = $3,885
Both television sets cost **$3,885**.

6.

girls | 3,865
boys | 1,459 | ?
?

$$\begin{array}{r} \overset{1}{3},\overset{1}{8}\overset{1}{6}5 \\ +\ 1,459 \\ \hline 5,324 \end{array}$$

3,865 + 1,459 = 5,324
5,324 boys went to the concert.

$$\begin{array}{r} \overset{1}{5},324 \\ +\ 3,865 \\ \hline 9,189 \end{array}$$

5,324 + 3,865 = 9,189
9,189 children went to the concert altogether.

7.

Saturday | 2,015
Sunday | 3,585 | ?
?

$$\begin{array}{r} 2,015 \\ +\ 3,585 \\ \hline 5,600 \end{array} \qquad \begin{array}{r} 5,600 \\ +\ 2,015 \\ \hline 7,615 \end{array}$$

2,015 + 3,585 = 5,600
5,600 people attended the carnival on Sunday.

5,600 + 2,015 = 7,615
7,615 people attended the carnival on both days.

8.

Monday | 1,075 kg
Tuesday | ? | 360 kg | ?

$$\begin{array}{r} \overset{0}{\cancel{1}},\overset{10}{\cancel{0}}75 \\ -\ \ 360 \\ \hline 715 \end{array} \qquad \begin{array}{r} 1,075 \\ +\ \ 715 \\ \hline 1,790 \end{array}$$

1,075 − 360 = 715
He used 715 kg of cement on Tuesday.

1,075 + 715 = 1,790
He used **1,790 kg** of cement on both days.

9. **(a)**

van | $5,180
motorcycle | $3,960 | ?

$$\begin{array}{r} \overset{4}{\cancel{5}},\overset{11}{\cancel{1}}80 \\ -\ 3,960 \\ \hline 1,220 \end{array}$$

$5,180 − $3,960 = $1,220
The used motorcycle is **$1,220** less than the used van.

(b)

$5,180 | $3,960
?

$$\begin{array}{r} \overset{1}{5},\overset{1}{1}80 \\ +\ 3,960 \\ \hline 9,140 \end{array}$$

$5,180 + $3,960 = $9,140

It will cost **$9,140** to buy the used van and the used motorcycle.

10. **(a)**

last year | $2,387
this year | ? | $500

$$\begin{array}{r} \overset{1}{\cancel{2}},\overset{13}{\cancel{3}}87 \\ -\ \ 500 \\ \hline 1,887 \end{array}$$

$2,387 − $500 = $1,887
Alexandra could spend **$1,887** on books and school supplies this year.

(b)

$4,000
$1,887 | ?

$$\begin{array}{r} \overset{3}{\cancel{4}},\overset{9}{\cancel{0}}\overset{9}{\cancel{0}}\overset{10}{\cancel{0}} \\ -\ 1,887 \\ \hline 2,113 \end{array}$$

$4,000 − $1,887 = $2,113
She would have overspent by **$2,113**.

Review 2

1.

$$\begin{array}{r} \overset{8}{\cancel{9}},\overset{13}{\cancel{3}}\overset{5}{\cancel{6}}\overset{18}{\cancel{8}} \\ -\ 1,409 \\ \hline 7,959 \end{array}$$

2.

$$\begin{array}{r} \overset{3}{\cancel{4}},\overset{16}{\cancel{7}}\overset{15}{\cancel{5}}5 \\ -\ 1,890 \\ \hline \mathbf{2,865} \end{array}$$

3.
$$
\begin{array}{r}
{}^{7}\ {}^{11}\\
8,\cancel{1}11\\
-\ 2,401\\
\hline
5,710\\
\end{array}
$$

4.
$$
\begin{array}{r}
{}^{5}\ {}^{9}\ {}^{9}\ {}^{10}\\
\cancel{6},\cancel{0}\cancel{0}\cancel{0}\\
-\ 2,819\\
\hline
3,181\\
\end{array}
$$

5. **3**
$$
\begin{array}{r}
{}^{1}\ {}^{1}\ {}^{1}\\
3,789\\
+\ 5,747\\
\hline
9,536\\
\end{array}
$$

6. **5**
$$
\begin{array}{r}
{}^{1}\\
1,173\\
+\ 4,371\\
\hline
5,544\\
\end{array}
$$

7. **4,217**
$$
\begin{array}{r}
{}^{5}\ {}^{15}\\
6,8\cancel{6}\cancel{5}\\
-\ 2,648\\
\hline
4,217\\
\end{array}
$$

8. **1,115**
$$
\begin{array}{r}
2,865\\
-\ 1,750\\
\hline
1,115\\
\end{array}
$$

9. **4,889**
$$
\begin{array}{r}
{}^{8}\ {}^{9}\ {}^{10}\\
5,\cancel{9}\cancel{0}\cancel{0}\\
-\ 1,011\\
\hline
4,889\\
\end{array}
$$

10. **3,900**
$$
\begin{array}{r}
{}^{3}\ {}^{10}\\
\cancel{4},\cancel{0}00\\
-\ \ \ \ 100\\
\hline
3,900\\
\end{array}
$$

11. **6,930**
$$
\begin{array}{r}
6,940\\
-\ \ \ \ \ 10\\
\hline
6,930\\
\end{array}
$$

12. **7,550**
$$
\begin{array}{r}
{}^{7}\ {}^{9}\ {}^{10}\\
\cancel{8},\cancel{0}\cancel{0}0\\
-\ \ \ \ 450\\
\hline
7,550\\
\end{array}
$$

13. **5,550**
$$
\begin{array}{r}
5,050\\
+\ \ \ 500\\
\hline
5,550\\
\end{array}
$$

14.
R
$$
\begin{array}{r}
{}^{5}\ {}^{12}\ {}^{18}\\
\cancel{6},\cancel{3}\cancel{8}9\\
-\ 4,693\\
\hline
1,696\\
\end{array}
$$

T
$$
\begin{array}{r}
{}^{1}\ {}^{1}\ {}^{1}\\
2,415\\
+\ 1,596\\
\hline
4,011\\
\end{array}
$$

E
$$
\begin{array}{r}
{}^{7}\ {}^{11}\ {}^{9}\ {}^{10}\\
\cancel{8},\cancel{2}\cancel{0}\cancel{0}\\
-\ 3,865\\
\hline
4,335\\
\end{array}
$$

A
$$
\begin{array}{r}
{}^{1}\\
5,189\\
+\ 2,690\\
\hline
7,879\\
\end{array}
$$

U
$$
\begin{array}{r}
{}^{2}\ {}^{14}\ {}^{7}\ {}^{17}\\
\cancel{3},\cancel{4}\cancel{8}\cancel{7}\\
-\ 1,509\\
\hline
1,978\\
\end{array}
$$

B
$$
\begin{array}{r}
4,444\\
+\ 2,055\\
\hline
6,499\\
\end{array}
$$

N
$$
\begin{array}{r}
{}^{6}\ {}^{16}\ {}^{16}\ {}^{17}\\
\cancel{7},\cancel{7}\cancel{7}\cancel{7}\\
-\ 5,998\\
\hline
1,779\\
\end{array}
$$

P
$$
\begin{array}{r}
{}^{1}\\
1,090\\
+\ 2,895\\
\hline
3,985\\
\end{array}
$$

P	E	A	N	U	T
3,985	4,335	7,879	1,779	1,978	4,011

B	U	T	T	E	R
6,499	1,978	4,011	4,011	4,335	1,696

15. (a) Sophia $2,470 / June $2,745 ?
$$
\begin{array}{r}
{}^{6}\ {}^{14}\\
2,\cancel{7}\cancel{4}5\\
-\ 2,470\\
\hline
275\\
\end{array}
$$
$2,745 − $2,470 = $275
June earns **$275** more than Sophia.

(b) $2,745 | $2,470 ?
$$
\begin{array}{r}
{}^{1}\ {}^{1}\\
2,745\\
+\ 2,470\\
\hline
5,215\\
\end{array}
$$
$2,745 + $2,470 = $5,215
They earn **$5,215** altogether.

16. Yoko 2,100 / Andrew 1,900 ?
$$
\begin{array}{r}
{}^{1}\\
2,100\\
+\ 1,900\\
\hline
4,000\\
\end{array}
$$
2,100 + 1,900 = 4,000
Andrew has 4,000 stamps.
$$
\begin{array}{r}
4,000\\
+\ 2,100\\
\hline
6,100\\
\end{array}
$$
4,000 + 2,100 = 6,100
They have **6,100** stamps altogether.

17. A 4,985 / B ? 1,200 / C ? 2,350
$$
\begin{array}{r}
4,985\\
+\ 1,200\\
\hline
6,185\\
\end{array}
$$
4,985 + 1,200 = 6,185
Shop B sells 6,185 T-shirts.
$$
\begin{array}{r}
{}^{5}\ {}^{11}\\
\cancel{6},\cancel{1}85\\
-\ 2,350\\
\hline
3,835\\
\end{array}
$$
6,185 − 2,350 = 3,835
Shop C sells **3,835** T-shirts.

18. 3,967 | 450 ?
$$
\begin{array}{r}
{}^{1}\ {}^{1}\\
3,967\\
+\ \ \ 450\\
\hline
4,417\\
\end{array}
$$
3,967 + 450 = 4,417
Jake has 4,417 stickers.

? | 1,050 / 4,417
$$
\begin{array}{r}
{}^{3}\ {}^{11}\\
4,\cancel{4}\cancel{1}7\\
-\ 1,050\\
\hline
3,367\\
\end{array}
$$
4,417 − 1,050 = 3,367
Jake has **3,367** stickers left.

19. August 4,745 mi. / September ? 2,080 mi. ?
$$
\begin{array}{r}
{}^{6}\ {}^{14}\\
4,\cancel{7}\cancel{4}5\\
-\ 2,080\\
\hline
2,665\\
\end{array}
$$
4,745 − 2,080 = 2,665
He drove 2,665 km in September.
$$
\begin{array}{r}
{}^{1}\ {}^{1}\ {}^{1}\\
4,745\\
+\ 2,665\\
\hline
7,410\\
\end{array}
$$
4,745 + 2,665 = 7,410
Raj's total driving distance in these 2 months was **7,410 mi.**

20. (a) castle 5,000 / house ? 4,360
$$
\begin{array}{r}
{}^{4}\ {}^{9}\ {}^{10}\\
\cancel{5},\cancel{0}\cancel{0}0\\
-\ 4,360\\
\hline
640\\
\end{array}
$$
5,000 − 4,360 = 640
He used **640** wooden blocks to build the house.

(b) 5,000 | 640 ?
$$
\begin{array}{r}
5,000\\
+\ \ \ 640\\
\hline
5,640\\
\end{array}
$$
5,000 + 640 = 5,640
He used **5,640** wooden blocks altogether.

Singapore Math Practice Level 3A

Unit 5: Multiplying Numbers by 6, 7, 8, and 9

1. **12**
   6 + 6 = 12
2. **30**
   6 + 6 + 6 + 6 + 6 = 30
3. **10**
   8 + 8 + 8 + 8 + 8 + 8 + 8 + 8 + 8 + 8 = 80
4. **8**
   7 + 7 + 7 + 7 + 7 + 7 + 7 + 7 = 56
5. **81**
   9 + 9 + 9 + 9 + 9 + 9 + 9 + 9 + 9 = 81
6. **5**
   8 + 8 + 8 + 8 + 8 = 40
7. **32**
   8 + 8 + 8 + 8 = 32
8. **4**
   6 + 6 + 6 + 6 = 24
9. **21**
   7 + 7 + 7 = 21
10. **49**
    7 + 7 + 7 + 7 + 7 + 7 + 7 = 49
11. **45**
    9 + 9 + 9 + 9 + 9 = 45
12. **8**
    9 + 9 + 9 + 9 + 9 + 9 + 9 + 9 = 72
13. **8**
    8 + 8 + 8 + 8 + 8 + 8 + 8 + 8 = 64
14. **6**
    8 + 8 + 8 + 8 + 8 + 8 = 48
15. **0**
    Any number multiplied by 0 equals to 0.

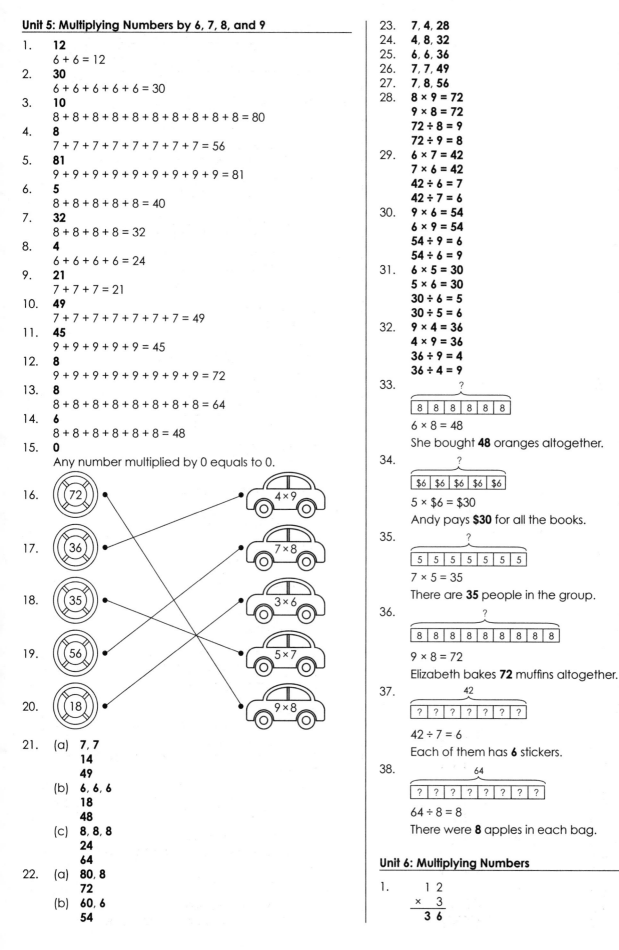

16. 72
17. 36
18. 35
19. 56
20. 18

16–20 matched to: 4 × 9, 7 × 8, 3 × 6, 5 × 7, 9 × 8

21. (a) **7, 7**
        14
        49
    (b) **6, 6, 6**
        18
        48
    (c) **8, 8, 8**
        24
        64
22. (a) **80, 8**
        72
    (b) **60, 6**
        54

23. **7, 4, 28**
24. **4, 8, 32**
25. **6, 6, 36**
26. **7, 7, 49**
27. **7, 8, 56**
28. **8 × 9 = 72**
    9 × 8 = 72
    72 ÷ 8 = 9
    72 ÷ 9 = 8
29. **6 × 7 = 42**
    7 × 6 = 42
    42 ÷ 6 = 7
    42 ÷ 7 = 6
30. **9 × 6 = 54**
    6 × 9 = 54
    54 ÷ 9 = 6
    54 ÷ 6 = 9
31. **6 × 5 = 30**
    5 × 6 = 30
    30 ÷ 6 = 5
    30 ÷ 5 = 6
32. **9 × 4 = 36**
    4 × 9 = 36
    36 ÷ 9 = 4
    36 ÷ 4 = 9
33.
    | ? |
    | 8 | 8 | 8 | 8 | 8 | 8 |

    6 × 8 = 48
    She bought **48** oranges altogether.
34.
    | ? |
    | $6 | $6 | $6 | $6 | $6 |

    5 × $6 = $30
    Andy pays **$30** for all the books.
35.
    | ? |
    | 5 | 5 | 5 | 5 | 5 | 5 | 5 |

    7 × 5 = 35
    There are **35** people in the group.
36.
    | ? |
    | 8 | 8 | 8 | 8 | 8 | 8 | 8 | 8 | 8 |

    9 × 8 = 72
    Elizabeth bakes **72** muffins altogether.
37.
    | 42 |
    | ? | ? | ? | ? | ? | ? | ? |

    42 ÷ 7 = 6
    Each of them has **6** stickers.
38.
    | 64 |
    | ? | ? | ? | ? | ? | ? | ? | ? |

    64 ÷ 8 = 8
    There were **8** apples in each bag.

Unit 6: Multiplying Numbers

1.   1 2
   ×   3
   ___
     3 6

111

Singapore Math Practice Level 3A

2.
```
  1 1 2
×     4
─────────
  4 4 8
```

3.
```
    3 3
×     2
───────
    6 6
```

4.
```
  2 1 0
×     2
─────────
  4 2 0
```

5.
```
  3 0 2
×     3
─────────
  9 0 6
```

6.
```
  4 4 2
×     2
─────────
  8 8 4
```

7.
```
  2 1 2
×     4
─────────
  8 4 8
```

8.
```
    3 1
×     3
───────
    9 3
```

9.
```
  1 0 0
×     3
─────────
  3 0 0
```

10.
```
  1 2 1
×     4
─────────
  4 8 4
```

11. 49 × 5

12. 147 × 4

13. 94 × 2

14. 231 × 7

15. 375 × 3

16. 105 × 8

188
```
   9 4
×    2
──────
 1 8 8
```

1,125
```
  ²3 ¹7 5
×      3
─────────
 1,1 2 5
```

840
```
  1 0 5
×     8
─────────
  8 4 0
```

245
```
    ⁴4 9
×      5
───────
  2 4 5
```

588
```
  ¹1 ²4 7
×      4
─────────
  5 8 8
```

1,617
```
  ²2 3 1
×      7
─────────
 1,6 1 7
```

17.

	(a) 8	9	(f) 6			(b) 7	1	1
(g) 6			(c) 3	1	0			
1			7			(h) 3		
2			(d) 8	5	6			
	(i) 8		(j) 6			(e) 8	2	6
	8		4					
	2		0					

(a)
```
  ¹1 1 2
×      8
─────────
  8 9 6
```

(f)
```
    9 1
×     7
───────
  6 3 7
```

(b)
```
   ⁸7 9
×     9
───────
 7 1 1
```

(g)
```
  1 ¹0 2
×      6
─────────
  6 1 2
```

(c)
```
   ¹6 2
×     5
───────
 3 1 0
```

(h)
```
   ⁴4 6
×     8
───────
 3 6 8
```

(d)
```
  2 ¹1 4
×      4
─────────
  8 5 6
```

(i)
```
   ⁷9 8
×     9
───────
 8 8 2
```

(e)
```
  ¹1 ⁵1 8
×       7
─────────
  8 2 6
```

(j)
```
    8 0
×     8
───────
  6 4 0
```

18.
```
  ²5 ³3 7
×       6
─────────
  3,2 2 2
```
```
  4 ³1 6
×      5
─────────
  2,0 8 0
```
```
  ²1 ²3 3
×       7
─────────
    9 3 1
```
```
  6 0 0
×     2
─────────
  1,2 0 0
```
```
  ²2 0 4
×      5
─────────
  1,0 2 0
```

```
  ¹7 ¹4 3
×       4
─────────
  2,9 7 2
```
```
  ⁷3 9 1
×      8
─────────
  3,1 2 8
```
```
  ⁶1 ⁸6 9
×       9
─────────
  1,5 2 1
```
```
  8 ¹2 4
×      3
─────────
  2,4 7 2
```

B	**O**	**B**	**O**		**T**	**H**	**E**
1,200	2,080	1,200	2,080		3,128	3,222	1,020

C	**L**	**O**	**W**	**N**
2,472	2,972	2,080	931	1,521

19.
```
              ?
┌──┬──┬──┬──┬──┬──┐
│15│15│15│15│15│15│
└──┴──┴──┴──┴──┴──┘
```
```
  ³1 5
×    6
──────
  9 0
```
6 × 15 = 90
There were **90** colored pencils altogether.

20.
```
       ?
┌────┬────┬────┐
│230 │230 │230 │
└────┴────┴────┘
```
```
  2 3 0
×     3
─────────
  6 9 0
```
230 × 3 = 690
The total number of people who went to the concert was **690**.

21.
```
        ?
┌─────┬─────┬─────┐
│$637 │$637 │$637 │
└─────┴─────┴─────┘
```
```
  ¹6 ²3 7
×       3
─────────
  1,9 1 1
```
$637 × 3 = $1,911
He spent **$1,911** at the electronics store.

22.
```
                    ?
┌──────┬──────┬──────┬──────┬──────┐
│750 mL│750 mL│750 mL│750 mL│750 mL│
└──────┴──────┴──────┴──────┴──────┘
```
```
  ²7 5 0
×      5
─────────
  3,7 5 0
```
750 × 5 = 3,750

112

Singapore Math Practice Level 3A

The total volume of syrup that Brittany bought was **3,750 mL**.

23.

$153 \times 4 = 612$
There were **612** wheels altogether.

$$\begin{array}{r} {}^{2}1\,{}^{1}5\,3 \\ \times \qquad 4 \\ \hline 6\,1\,2 \end{array}$$

Review 3

1. $5 \times 8 = 40$
   $8 \times 5 = 40$
   $40 \div 5 = 8$
   $40 \div 8 = 5$
2. $7 \times 4 = 28$
   $4 \times 7 = 28$
   $28 \div 7 = 4$
   $28 \div 4 = 7$
3. $$\begin{array}{r} {}^{3}1\,{}^{5}4\,7 \\ \times \qquad 8 \\ \hline 1,1\,7\,6 \end{array}$$
4. $$\begin{array}{r} 3\,1\,2 \\ \times \qquad 3 \\ \hline 9\,3\,6 \end{array}$$
5. $$\begin{array}{r} {}^{1}6\,3\,2 \\ \times \qquad 4 \\ \hline 2,5\,2\,8 \end{array}$$
6. $$\begin{array}{r} 5\,0\,0 \\ \times \qquad 3 \\ \hline 1,5\,0\,0 \end{array}$$
7. **5, 9, 45**
8.

13. **54**
    $6 + 6 + 6 + 6 + 6 + 6 + 6 + 6 + 6 = 54$
14. **7**
    $8 + 8 + 8 + 8 + 8 + 8 + 8 = 56$
15. **7**
    $7 + 7 + 7 + 7 = 28$
16. **7**
    $9 + 9 + 9 + 9 + 9 + 9 + 9 = 63$
17.

$139 \times 8 = 1,112$
She needs **1,112** beads to make 8 such bags.

$$\begin{array}{r} {}^{3}1\,{}^{7}3\,9 \\ \times \qquad 8 \\ \hline 1,1\,1\,2 \end{array}$$

18.

$235 \times 7 = 1,645$
He has **1,645** stamps altogether.

$$\begin{array}{r} {}^{2}2\,{}^{3}3\,5 \\ \times \qquad 7 \\ \hline 1,6\,4\,5 \end{array}$$

19.

$54 \div 9 = 6$
There were **6** ribbons in each packet.

20.

$45 \times 5 = 225$
45 cars can transport **225** people.

$$\begin{array}{r} {}^{2}4\,5 \\ \times \qquad 5 \\ \hline 2\,2\,5 \end{array}$$

Unit 7: Dividing Numbers

1. **9, 4**
   $$\begin{array}{r} 9 \\ 7\overline{)6\,7} \\ 6\,3 \\ \hline 4 \end{array}$$
2. **3, 2**
   $$\begin{array}{r} 3 \\ 5\overline{)1\,7} \\ 1\,5 \\ \hline 2 \end{array}$$
3. **8, 1**
   $$\begin{array}{r} 8 \\ 3\overline{)2\,5} \\ 2\,4 \\ \hline 1 \end{array}$$
4. **9, 7**
   $$\begin{array}{r} 9 \\ 9\overline{)8\,8} \\ 8\,1 \\ \hline 7 \end{array}$$
5. **7, 1**
   $$\begin{array}{r} 7 \\ 4\overline{)2\,9} \\ 2\,8 \\ \hline 1 \end{array}$$
6. **8, 4**
   $$\begin{array}{r} 8 \\ 6\overline{)5\,2} \\ 4\,8 \\ \hline 4 \end{array}$$
7. **234, 1**
   $$\begin{array}{r} 2\,3\,4 \\ 2\overline{)4\,6\,9} \\ 4 \\ \hline 6 \\ 6 \\ \hline 9 \\ 8 \\ \hline 1 \end{array}$$

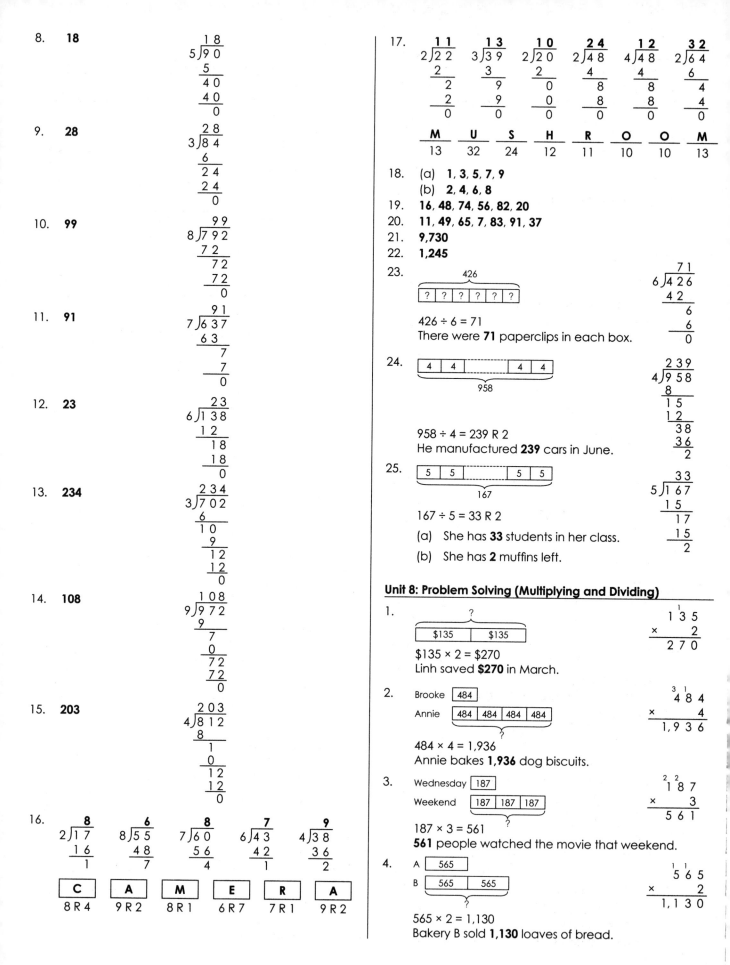

8. **18**

```
    1 8
5 ) 9 0
    5
    4 0
    4 0
      0
```

9. **28**

```
    2 8
3 ) 8 4
    6
    2 4
    2 4
      0
```

10. **99**

```
      9 9
8 ) 7 9 2
    7 2
      7 2
      7 2
        0
```

11. **91**

```
      9 1
7 ) 6 3 7
    6 3
        7
        7
        0
```

12. **23**

```
      2 3
6 ) 1 3 8
    1 2
      1 8
      1 8
        0
```

13. **234**

```
      2 3 4
3 ) 7 0 2
    6
    1 0
      9
      1 2
      1 2
        0
```

14. **108**

```
      1 0 8
9 ) 9 7 2
    9
    7
    0
      7 2
      7 2
        0
```

15. **203**

```
      2 0 3
4 ) 8 1 2
    8
    1
    0
      1 2
      1 2
        0
```

16.
```
    8        6        8        7        9
2 )1 7    8 )5 5    7 )6 0    6 )4 3    4 )3 8
  1 6        4 8      5 6        4 2        3 6
    1          7        4          1          2
```

C	A	M	E	R	A
8 R 4	9 R 2	8 R 1	6 R 7	7 R 1	9 R 2

17.
```
    1 1      1 3      1 0      2 4      1 2      3 2
2 )2 2    3 )3 9    2 )2 0    2 )4 8    4 )4 8    2 )6 4
  2          3        2          4        4          6
  2          9        0          8        8          4
  2          9                   8        8          4
  0          0        0          0        0          0
```

M	U	S	H	R	O	O	M
13	32	24	12	11	10	10	13

18. (a) **1, 3, 5, 7, 9**
     (b) **2, 4, 6, 8**

19. **16, 48, 74, 56, 82, 20**

20. **11, 49, 65, 7, 83, 91, 37**

21. **9,730**

22. **1,245**

23.

426

?	?	?	?	?	?

```
      7 1
6 ) 4 2 6
    4 2
        6
        6
        0
```

$426 \div 6 = 71$
There were **71** paperclips in each box.

24.

4	4	...	4	4

958

```
      2 3 9
4 ) 9 5 8
    8
    1 5
    1 2
      3 8
      3 6
        2
```

$958 \div 4 = 239 \text{ R } 2$
He manufactured **239** cars in June.

25.

5	5	...	5	5

167

```
      3 3
5 ) 1 6 7
    1 5
      1 7
      1 5
        2
```

$167 \div 5 = 33 \text{ R } 2$
(a) She has **33** students in her class.
(b) She has **2** muffins left.

Unit 8: Problem Solving (Multiplying and Dividing)

1.

?

$135	$135

$\$135 \times 2 = \$270$
Linh saved **$270** in March.

```
  1
  1 3 5
×     2
  2 7 0
```

2.

Brooke | 484 |

Annie | 484 | 484 | 484 | 484 |
?

$484 \times 4 = 1,936$
Annie bakes **1,936** dog biscuits.

```
  3 1
  4 8 4
×     4
1,9 3 6
```

3.

Wednesday | 187 |

Weekend | 187 | 187 | 187 |
?

$187 \times 3 = 561$
561 people watched the movie that weekend.

```
  2 2
  1 8 7
×     3
  5 6 1
```

4.

A | 565 |

B | 565 | 565 |
?

$565 \times 2 = 1,130$
Bakery B sold **1,130** loaves of bread.

```
  1 1
  5 6 5
×     2
1,1 3 0
```

5.

$?$: 25 | 25 | 25 | 25 | 25 | 25 | 25 | 25

$25 \times 8 = 200$

He bought **200** baseball cards altogether.

$$\begin{array}{r} \overset{4}{2}5 \\ \times\quad 8 \\ \hline 200 \end{array}$$

6.

1,506: ? | ? | ?

$1,506 \div 3 = 502$

He could put **502** fish into each pond.

$$\begin{array}{r} 502 \\ 3\overline{)1506} \\ \underline{15} \\ 0 \\ \underline{0} \\ 6 \\ \underline{6} \\ 0 \end{array}$$

7.

$516: ? | ? | ? | ? | ? | ?

$516 \div 6 = 86

Alex spent **$86** on transportation each month.

$$\begin{array}{r} 86 \\ 6\overline{)516} \\ \underline{48} \\ 36 \\ \underline{36} \\ 0 \end{array}$$

8.

8 | 8 | --- | 8 | 8
679

$679 \div 8 = 84\,R\,7$

(a) Keiko can make **84** rings.

(b) **7** beads are left.

$$\begin{array}{r} 84 \\ 8\overline{)679} \\ \underline{64} \\ 39 \\ \underline{32} \\ 7 \end{array}$$

9.

Hasaan | $1,375
John | ? | $70
Luis | _____ | ?

(a) $1,375 - $70 = $1,305$
John earns **$1,305**.

(b) $1,305 \times 2 = $2,610$
Luis earns **$2,610**.

$$\begin{array}{r} 1,375 \\ -\quad 70 \\ \hline 1,305 \end{array}$$

$$\begin{array}{r} 1,3\overset{1}{0}5 \\ \times\quad\quad 2 \\ \hline 2,610 \end{array}$$

10.

girls | 425
boys | 425 | 425 }?

(a) $425 \times 2 = 850$
There are **850** boys.

(b) $850 + 425 = 1,275$
There are **1,275** students altogether.

$$\begin{array}{r} 4\overset{1}{2}5 \\ \times\quad 2 \\ \hline 850 \end{array}$$

$$\begin{array}{r} 850 \\ +\quad 425 \\ \hline 1,275 \end{array}$$

11. (a)

last month | 312
this month | 312 | 68 }?

$312 + 68 = 380$
Sean collected **380** stamps this month.

(b)
380: ? | ?

$380 \div 2 = 190$
Each friend would get **190** stamps.

$$\begin{array}{r} 3\overset{1}{1}2 \\ +\quad 68 \\ \hline 380 \end{array}$$

$$\begin{array}{r} 190 \\ 2\overline{)380} \\ \underline{2} \\ 18 \\ \underline{18} \\ 0 \\ \underline{0} \\ 0 \end{array}$$

12. (a)

Lauren | $175
Jade | $159 }?

$175 - $159 = 16
Lauren spends **$16** more than Jade on food.

$$\begin{array}{r} \overset{6}{1}\,\overset{15}{\cancel{7}}\,5 \\ -\quad 59 \\ \hline 16 \end{array}$$

(b)

$?: $16 | $16 | $16 | $16 | $16 | $16

$16 \times 6 = 96
Lauren spends **$96** more on food than Jade in 6 months.

$$\begin{array}{r} \overset{3}{1}6 \\ \times\quad 6 \\ \hline 96 \end{array}$$

13. (a)

$?: 98 | 98

$98 \times 2 = 196$
Mr. McKay travels **196 km** to and from the city.

$$\begin{array}{r} \overset{1}{9}8 \\ \times\quad 2 \\ \hline 196 \end{array}$$

(b)

$?: 196 | 196 | 196 | 196 | 196 | 196 | 196

$196 \times 7 = 1,372$
He will travel **1,372 km** in all.

$$\begin{array}{r} \overset{6}{1}\overset{4}{9}6 \\ \times\quad 7 \\ \hline 1,372 \end{array}$$

14. (a)

$?: $160 | $160 | $160 | $160 | $160 | $160

$160 \times 6 = 960
Emelda saved **$960** in half a year.

$$\begin{array}{r} \overset{3}{1}60 \\ \times\quad 6 \\ \hline 960 \end{array}$$

(b)

$960: ? | ? | ? | ? | ? | ? | ? | ?

$960 \div 8 = 120
The cost of each present was **$120**.

$$\begin{array}{r} 120 \\ 8\overline{)960} \\ \underline{8} \\ 16 \\ \underline{16} \\ 0 \\ \underline{0} \\ 0 \end{array}$$

15. (a)

$?: 6 | 6 | 6 | 6 | 6 | 6 | 6 | 6

$6 \times 8 = 48$
She uses **48 yd.** of fabric in a week.

(b)

100 yds.: 48 | ?

$100 - 48 = 52$
She has **52 yd.** of fabric left.

$$\begin{array}{r} \overset{0}{\cancel{1}}\overset{9}{\cancel{0}}\overset{10}{\cancel{0}} \\ -\quad 48 \\ \hline 52 \end{array}$$

16.

$?: 25 | 25 | 25 | 25 | 25 | 25 | 25 | 25 | 25

$25 \times 9 = 225$
There were 225 crayons altogether.

5 | 5 | --- | 5 | 5
225

$225 \div 5 = 45$
She had **45** students.

$$\begin{array}{r} \overset{4}{2}5 \\ \times\quad 9 \\ \hline 225 \end{array}$$

$$\begin{array}{r} 45 \\ 5\overline{)225} \\ \underline{20} \\ 25 \\ \underline{25} \\ 0 \end{array}$$

17.

$?: 24 | 24 | 24

$24 \times 3 = 72$
There were 72 apples altogether.

$?: 72 | 245

$72 + 245 = 317$
She bought **317** pieces of fruit altogether.

$$\begin{array}{r} \overset{1}{2}4 \\ \times\quad 3 \\ \hline 72 \end{array}$$

$$\begin{array}{r} \overset{1}{2}45 \\ +\quad 72 \\ \hline 317 \end{array}$$

18.

radio | $95 | $95 }?
TV | $190

$95 \times 2 = 190
$190 \times 2 = 380
He needs **$380**.

$$\begin{array}{r} \overset{1}{9}5 \\ \times\quad 2 \\ \hline 190 \end{array}\qquad \begin{array}{r} \overset{1}{1}90 \\ \times\quad 2 \\ \hline 380 \end{array}$$

115

19.

chair $75
table $75 $75 $75 } ?

$$\begin{array}{r} {}^{2}75 \\ \times\ \ \ 4 \\ \hline 300 \end{array}$$

$75 × 4 = $300
Charley paid **$300** for the furniture.

20.

English
math } 171

$$3\overline{\smash{)}171}$$ with work showing $171 ÷ 3 = 57$

$$\begin{array}{r} 57 \\ 3\overline{\smash{)}171} \\ 15 \\ \hline 21 \\ 21 \\ \hline 0 \end{array}$$

$$\begin{array}{r} {}^{1}57 \\ \times\ \ \ 2 \\ \hline 114 \end{array}$$

$171 ÷ 3 = 57$
$57 × 2 = 114$
She scored **114** points in English.

Unit 9: Mental Calculations

1. **89**
    $65 + 20 = 85$
    $85 + 4 = 89$
2. **52**
    $40 + 13 = 53$
    $53 - 1 = 52$
3. **134**
    $56 + 80 = 136$
    $136 - 2 = 134$
4. **128**
    $84 + 40 = 124$
    $124 + 4 = 128$
5. **99**
    $74 + 20 = 94$
    $94 + 5 = 99$
6. **118**
    $31 + 80 = 111$
    $111 + 7 = 118$
7. **90**
    $42 + 50 = 92$
    $92 - 2 = 0$
8. **158**
    $61 + 100 = 161$
    $161 - 3 = 158$
9. **86**
    $57 + 30 = 87$
    $87 - 1 = 86$
10. **77**
    $20 + 58 = 78$
    $78 - 1 = 77$
11. **31**
    $49 - 10 = 39$
    $39 - 8 = 31$
12. **21**
    $74 - 50 = 24$
    $24 - 3 = 21$
13. **45**
    $64 - 20 = 44$
    $44 + 1 = 45$
14. **55**
    $83 - 30 = 53$
    $53 + 2 = 55$
15. **28**
    $37 - 10 = 27$
    $27 + 1 = 28$
16. **39**
    $86 - 50 = 36$
    $36 + 3 = 39$
17. **27**
    $62 - 40 = 22$
    $22 + 5 = 27$
18. **31**
    $77 - 50 = 27$
    $27 + 4 = 31$
19. **49**
    $96 - 50 = 46$
    $46 + 3 = 49$
20. **28**
    $55 - 30 = 25$
    $25 + 3 = 28$
21. **40**
22. **81**
23. **21**
24. **18**
25. **28**
26. **18**
27. **480**
    $8 × 6$ tens $= 48$ tens $= 480$
28. **420**
    $6 × 7$ tens $= 42$ tens $= 420$
29. **1,200**
    $3 × 4$ hundreds $=$
    12 hundreds $= 1,200$
30. **2,500**
    $5 × 5$ hundreds $=$
    25 hundreds $= 2,500$
31. **8**
    $3 × 8 = 24$
32. **9**
    $6 × 9 = 54$
33. **10**
    $5 × 10 = 50$
34. **9**
    $8 × 9 = 72$
35. **10**
    $10 × 9 = 90$
36. **20**
    8 tens $÷ 4 = 2$ tens $= 20$
37. **50**
    35 tens $÷ 7 = 5$ tens $= 50$
38. **70**
    21 tens $÷ 3 = 7$ tens $= 70$
39. **60**
    36 tens $÷ 6 = 6$ tens $= 60$
40. **40**
    16 tens $÷ 4 = 4$ tens $= 40$

Review 4

1. **76, 5**

$$\begin{array}{r} 76 \\ 7\overline{\smash{)}537} \\ 49 \\ \hline 47 \\ 42 \\ \hline 5 \end{array}$$

116

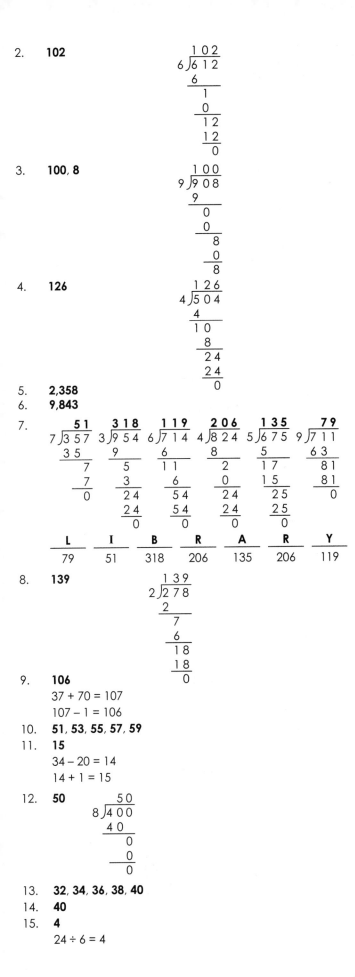

2. **102**

3. **100**, **8**

4. **126**

5. **2,358**
6. **9,843**
7.

	L	I	B	R	A	R	Y
	79	51	318	206	135	206	119

8. **139**

9. **106**

   $37 + 70 = 107$

   $107 - 1 = 106$

10. **51**, **53**, **55**, **57**, **59**
11. **15**

   $34 - 20 = 14$

   $14 + 1 = 15$

12. **50**

13. **32**, **34**, **36**, **38**, **40**
14. **40**
15. **4**

   $24 \div 6 = 4$

16. (a)

   $4 \times 5 = 20$

   There are **20** packets of noodles altogether.

   (b)

   $20 \div 2 = 10$

   She gives the noodles to **10** friends.

17.

   $230 \times 6 = 1,380$

   There are **1,380** stamps altogether.

   $1,380 \div 3 = 460$

   Each nephew receives **460** stamps.

18.

   $50 \times 4 = 200$

   She needs **200 g** of sugar for each loaf of banana bread.

19.

   $\$27 \div 3 = \$9$

   $\$40 \div 5 = \$8$

   Shop B sells the toy at a cheaper price.

20. (a)

   $464 \div 2 = 232$

   Nick's house is **232 yd.** from the city.

   (b)

   $464 \times 5 = 2,320$

   Nick would travel **2,320 yd.** in 5 days.

Final Review

1. **7,300**
2. **4,040**
3. **five thousand, fifteen**
4. **six thousand, four hundred eleven**
5.

Singapore Math Practice Level 3A

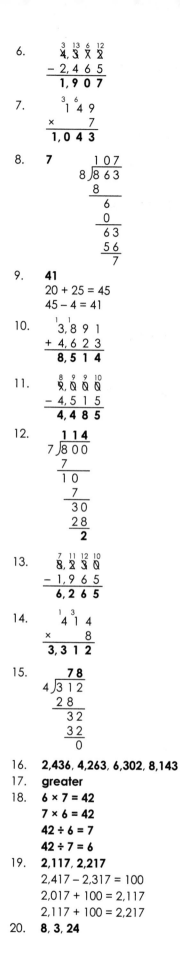

6.
$$\begin{array}{r} \overset{3}{\cancel{4}}\,\overset{13}{\cancel{3}}\,\overset{6}{\cancel{7}}\,\overset{12}{\cancel{2}} \\ -\ 2{,}4\ 6\ 5 \\ \hline 1{,}9\ 0\ 7 \end{array}$$

7.
$$\begin{array}{r} \overset{3}{1}\overset{6}{4}\,9 \\ \times\ \ \ \ 7 \\ \hline 1{,}0\ 4\ 3 \end{array}$$

8.
7
$$\begin{array}{r} 1\,0\,7 \\ 8\,\overline{)8\,6\,3} \\ \underline{8} \\ 6 \\ \underline{0} \\ 6\,3 \\ \underline{5\,6} \\ 7 \end{array}$$

9. **41**
20 + 25 = 45
45 − 4 = 41

10.
$$\begin{array}{r} \overset{1}{3}{,}\overset{1}{8}\,9\,1 \\ +\ 4{,}6\,2\,3 \\ \hline 8{,}5\,1\,4 \end{array}$$

11.
$$\begin{array}{r} \overset{8}{\cancel{9}}\,\overset{9}{\cancel{0}}\,\overset{9}{\cancel{0}}\,\overset{10}{\cancel{0}} \\ -\ 4{,}5\,1\,5 \\ \hline 4{,}4\,8\,5 \end{array}$$

12.
$$\begin{array}{r} 1\,1\,4 \\ 7\,\overline{)8\,0\,0} \\ \underline{7} \\ 1\,0 \\ \underline{7} \\ 3\,0 \\ \underline{2\,8} \\ 2 \end{array}$$

13.
$$\begin{array}{r} \overset{7}{\cancel{8}}\,\overset{11}{\cancel{2}}\,\overset{12}{\cancel{3}}\,\overset{10}{\cancel{0}} \\ -\ 1{,}9\,6\,5 \\ \hline 6{,}2\,6\,5 \end{array}$$

14.
$$\begin{array}{r} \overset{1}{4}\,\overset{3}{1}\,4 \\ \times\ \ \ \ 8 \\ \hline 3{,}3\,1\,2 \end{array}$$

15.
$$\begin{array}{r} 7\,8 \\ 4\,\overline{)3\,1\,2} \\ \underline{2\,8} \\ 3\,2 \\ \underline{3\,2} \\ 0 \end{array}$$

16. **2,436, 4,263, 6,302, 8,143**
17. **greater**
18. **6 × 7 = 42**
    7 × 6 = 42
    42 ÷ 6 = 7
    42 ÷ 7 = 6
19. **2,117, 2,217**
    2,417 − 2,317 = 100
    2,017 + 100 = 2,117
    2,117 + 100 = 2,217
20. **8, 3, 24**

21.
$$55 \times 8 = 440$$
$$\begin{array}{r} \overset{4}{5}5 \\ \times\ \ 8 \\ \hline 4\,4\,0 \end{array}\qquad \begin{array}{r} 2\,2\,0 \\ 2\,\overline{)4\,4\,0} \\ \underline{4} \\ 4 \\ \underline{4} \\ 0 \\ \underline{0} \\ 0 \end{array}$$
There are 440 seashells altogether.

$$440 \div 2 = 220$$
There are **220** seashells in each bag.

22.
Carson | 316
James | 316 | 316 | 316
Dan | ? | 400

$$316 \times 3 = 948$$
$$948 - 400 = 548$$
Dan has **548** bottle caps.

$$\begin{array}{r} 3\overset{1}{1}6 \\ \times\ \ \ 3 \\ \hline 9\,4\,8 \end{array}$$
$$\begin{array}{r} 9\,4\,8 \\ -\ 4\,0\,0 \\ \hline 5\,4\,8 \end{array}$$

23. (a)
1,416 yd. | 165 yd.
$$1{,}416 + 165 = 1{,}581$$
The shop is **1,581 yd.** away from her house.

$$\begin{array}{r} 1\,4\overset{1}{1}6 \\ +\ \ 1\,6\,5 \\ \hline 1{,}5\,8\,1 \end{array}$$

(b)
1,581 yd. | 1,581 yd.
$$1{,}581 \times 2 = 3{,}162$$
She walks **3,162 yd.**

$$\begin{array}{r} \overset{1}{1}\overset{1}{5}\,8\,1 \\ \times\ \ \ \ 2 \\ \hline 3{,}1\,6\,2 \end{array}$$

24.
138 km
? | ?
$$138 \div 2 = 69$$
She will travel **69 km.**

$$\begin{array}{r} 6\,9 \\ 2\,\overline{)1\,3\,8} \\ \underline{1\,2} \\ 1\,8 \\ \underline{1\,8} \\ 0 \end{array}$$

25.
$1,450 | $1,450
$$\$1{,}450 \times 2 = \$2{,}900$$
Monica paid $2,900 for the entertainment center.

$$\begin{array}{r} 1\,4\overset{1}{5}0 \\ \times\ \ \ \ 2 \\ \hline 2{,}9\,0\,0 \end{array}$$

$5,000
$2,900 | $1,450 | ?

$$\$2{,}900 + \$1{,}450 = \$4{,}350$$
$$\$5{,}000 - \$4{,}350 = \$650$$
She would receive **$650** in change.

$$\begin{array}{r} \overset{1}{2}{,}9\,0\,0 \\ +\ 1{,}4\,5\,0 \\ \hline 4{,}3\,5\,0 \end{array}$$

$$\begin{array}{r} \overset{4}{\cancel{5}}{,}\overset{9}{\cancel{0}}\,\overset{10}{\cancel{0}}\,0 \\ -\ 4{,}3\,5\,0 \\ \hline 6\,5\,0 \end{array}$$

Challenge Questions

1. $6 + $12 + $18 + $24 + $30 + $36 + $42 = $168
   He will save **$168** by Sunday.

2. Starting from the third term, the result of each term is obtained by adding its 2 preceding numbers.
   47 + 29 = **76**
   76 + 47 = **123**
   123 + 76 = **199**

Singapore Math Practice Level 3A

3.

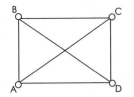

A shook hands with B, C, and D. (3 handshakes)

B shook hands with C and D. (2 handshakes)

C shook hands with D. (1 handshake)

3 + 2 + 1 = 6 handshakes

4 people were at the party.

4. The possible combinations of the 2-digit numbers are 12, 13, 21, 23, 31, and 32.

The 2-digit numbers that can be divided by 4 are **12** and **32**.

5. Let the digits be A, B, C, and D.

$$\underline{\ \ A\ \ } \quad \underline{\underset{\text{smallest}}{\ \ B\ \ }} \quad \underline{\underset{\text{biggest}}{\ \ C\ \ }} \quad \underline{\ \ D\ \ }$$

(C + D) – (A + B) = 8

A + B + C + D = 26

Use the guess-and-check method.

C + D = 9 + 8 = 17

A + B = 5 + 4 = 9

17 – 9 = 8

5 + 4 + 9 + 8 = 26

Number X is **5,498**.

6. When divided by 5, the number could be 22, 27, ㉜, or 37.

When divided by 6, the number could be 26, ㉜, or 38.

32 ÷ 5 = 6 R 2

32 ÷ 6 = 5 R 2

I am **32**.

7.

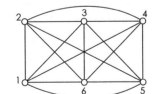

2, 6, 10, 15, 20, 24, **28**, **33**, 38, 42, **46**, **51**

8.

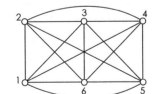

1st person exchanged handshakes with 5 other people.

2nd person exchanged handshakes with 4 other people.

3rd person exchanged handshakes with 3 other people.

4th person exchanged handshakes with 2 other people.

5th person exchanged handshakes with 1 other person.

5 + 4 + 3 + 2 + 1 = 15

15 handshakes were exchanged.

9. When shared by 3 boys, the number of peaches could be 4, 7, 10, ⑬, 16, or 19.

When shared by 4 boys, the number of peaches could be 5, 9, ⑬, or 17.

13 ÷ 3 = 4 R 1

13 ÷ 4 = 3 R 1

There are **13** peaches in the bag.

10. A = C

B – A = 1

A + B + C = 4

Using the guess-and-check method:

2 – 1 = 1

1 + 2 + 1 = 4

The 3-digit odd number is **121**.

11. 44 – 32 = 12

56 – 44 = 12

68 – 56 = 12

68 + 12 = 80

10 workers need **80** days to build the same building.

12. 3 × 7 = 21

21 × 5 = 105

The sum of the facing page numbers is 105.

52 + 53 = 105

The facing page numbers are **52** and **53**.

Notes

Notes

Notes

Notes

Singapore Math Practice Level 3A

Notes

Notes

Notes